IDENTITY THEFT

IDENTITY THEFT

CLAUDIA L. HAYWARD
EDITOR

Novinka Books
New York

Senior Editors: Susan Boriotti and Donna Dennis
Coordinating Editor: Tatiana Shohov
Office Manager: Annette Hellinger
Graphics: Wanda Serrano and Matt Dallow
Editorial Production: Alexandra Columbus, Maya Columbus, Alexis Klestov,
  Vladimir Klestov, Matthew Kozlowski and Lorna Loperfido
Circulation: Ave Maria Gonzalez, Vera Popovic, Luis Aviles, Sean Corkery,
  Raymond Davis, Melissa Diaz, Meagan Flaherty, Magdalena Nuñez,
  Marlene Nuñez, Jeannie Pappas and Frankie Punger
Communications and Acquisitions: Serge P. Shohov
Marketing: Cathy DeGregory

Library of Congress Cataloging-in-Publication Data
Available Upon Request

ISBN: 1-59033-878-2.

Copyright © 2004 by Novinka Books, An Imprint of
  Nova Science Publishers, Inc.
  400 Oser Ave, Suite 1600
  Hauppauge, New York 11788-3619
  Tele. 631-231-7269   Fax 631-231-8175
  e-mail: Novascience@earthlink.net
  Web Site: http://www.novapublishers.com

All rights reserved. No part of this book may be reproduced, stored in a retrieval system or transmitted in any form or by any means: electronic, electrostatic, magnetic, tape, mechanical photocopying, recording or otherwise without permission from the publishers.

The authors and publisher have taken care in preparation of this book, but make no expressed or implied warranty of any kind and assume no responsibility for any errors or omissions. No liability is assumed for incidental or consequential damages in connection with or arising out of information contained in this book.

This publication is designed to provide accurate and authoritative information with regard to the subject matter covered herein. It is sold with the clear understanding that the publisher is not engaged in rendering legal or any other professional services. If legal or any other expert assistance is required, the services of a competent person should be sought. FROM A DECLARATION OF PARTICIPANTS JOINTLY ADOPTED BY A COMMITTEE OF THE AMERICAN BAR ASSOCIATION AND A COMMITTEE OF PUBLISHERS.

Printed in the United States of America

CONTENTS

Foreword		vii
Chapter 1	Identity Theft: An Overview of Proposed Legislation *Angie A. Welborn*	1
Chapter 2	Identity Theft: Prevalence and Cost Appear to be Growing *Richard M. Stana*	17
Chapter 3	Remedies Available to Victims of Identity Theft *Angie A. Welborn*	73
Chapter 4	Financial Privacy Laws Affecting Sharing of Customer Information Among Affiliated Institutions *M. Maureen Murphy*	85
Chapter 5	Awareness and Use of Existing Data on Identity Theft *Richard M. Stana*	93
Chapter 6	Identity Theft and the Fair Credit Reporting Act: An Analysis of *TRW v. Andrews* and Current Legislation *Angie A. Welborn*	129
Chapter 7	Privacy Protection for Customer Financial Information *M. Maureen Murphy*	137
Chapter 8	Social Security Identity Theft Fact Sheet	145
Index		151

FOREWORD

Crime has moved yet another step forward in its unyielding progression through society. Now it is identity theft. Trying to combat both legal and illegal theft continues to occupy a large portion of the average citizen's life. Identity theft or identity fraud generally involves "stealing" another person's personal identifying information - such as Social Security number (SSN), date of birth, and mother's maiden name - and then using the information to fraudulently establish credit, run up debt, or take over existing financial accounts. This new book examines the extent of the problem, its costs and remedies under the law.

Chapter one provides an overview of legislation proposed during the 107th Congress to address the growing problem of identify theft. Most of the legislation from the 107th Congress sought to prevent identify theft through a variety of measures, including placing limitations on the use of social security numbers, requiring the truncation of credit card numbers, and placing additional limitations on access to consumer credit reports. Legislation was also introduced aimed at assisting victims with the oftentimes arduous task of removing information resulting from identity theft from their credit reports, and providing greater criminal penalties for those convicted of identity theft and related crimes. The bills are arranged by chamber and presented in numerical order.

Identity theft involves "stealing" another person's personal identifying information, such as their Social Security number (SSN), date of birth, or mother's maiden name, and using that information to fraudulently establish credit, run up debt, or take over existing financial accounts. Precise, statistical measurement of identity theft trends is difficult for several reasons. Federal law enforcement agencies lack information systems to track identity theft cases. Also, identity theft is almost always a component of one or more white-collar or financial crimes, such as bank fraud, credit card or access device fraud, or the use of counterfeit financial instruments. Data sources, such as consumer complaints and hotline allegations, can be used as proxies for gauging the prevalence of identity theft. Law enforcement investigations and prosecutions of bank and credit card fraud also provide data. Chapter two shows the estimates of the cost of identity theft to the financial services industry. Some data on identity theft-related losses indicated increasing costs. Other data, such as staffing of the fraud departments of banks and consumer reporting agencies, presented a mixed or incomplete picture. Identity theft can cause victims severe emotional and economic harm, including bounced checks, loan denials, and debt collection harassment. The federal criminal justice system incurs costs associated with investigations, prosecutions, incarceration, and community supervision.

Chapter three provides an overview of the federal laws that could assist victims of identity theft with purging inaccurate information from their credit records and removing unauthorized changes from credit accounts, as well as federal laws that impost criminal penalties on those who assume another person's identity through the use of fraudulent identification documents. State laws and recent legislative proposals aimed at preventing identity theft and providing additional remedies are also discussed.

Chapter four provides an analysis of the current federal law and a description of state laws that appear to provide more consumer protection with respect to the issue of information sharing among affiliates.

Identity theft or identity fraud generally involves "stealing" another person's personal identifying information--such as Social Security Number (SSN), date of birth, and mother's maiden name--and then using the information to fraudulently establish credit, run up debt, or take away existing financial accounts. The Identity Theft and Assumption Deterrence Act of 1998 made identity theft a separate crime against the person whose identity was stolen, broadened the scope of the offense to include the misuse of information as well as documents and provided punishment-- generally a fine or imprisonment or both. Chapter five shows (1) SSN misuse and (2) program fraud with SSN misuse potential as well as examples of cases prosecuted under the Federal Identity Theft Act.

One of the ways in which victims of identify theft may recover for financial harm is by filing suit under the Fair Credit Reporting Act. However, the Act imposes a two-year statute of limitations on suits filed. On November 13, 2001, the Supreme Court decided a case interpreting when the Act's statute of limitations begins to run. In that case, the Court held that the statute of limitations begins to run when inaccurate disclosures first occur, and not when the consumer learns of the inaccuracies in his report. Several pieces of legislation attempting to provide consumers with additional time to file suit have been introduced in response to the Court's decision. Chapter six provides a summary of the Fair Credit Reporting Act provisions in question, as well as an analysis of the recent Supreme Court decision and an overview of the legislation introduced in response to that decision.

Chapter seven discusses Title V of the Gramm-Leach-Bliley Act of 1999 (P.L. 106-102), H.Rept. 106-434) which requires financial institutions to provide their customers with notice of their privacy policies, including those relating to sharing of customer information with affiliated entities. It prohibits sharing personally identifiable information with non-affiliated third parties and prohibits financial institutions from providing account numbers to non-affiliated third parties for marketing purposes. it requires financial institutions to safeguard the security and confidentiality of customer information. It delegates rulemaking and enforcement authority to the various functional regulators of financial institutions.

Chapter 1

IDENTITY THEFT: AN OVERVIEW OF PROPOSED LEGISLATION[‡]

Angie A. Welborn

INTRODUCTION

During the 108th Congress, identity theft is likely to once again be a focus of the legislative agenda. Since the Federal Trade Commission first identified identity theft as the number one consumer complaint in 2000, problems associated with identity theft have grown. Despite efforts at the state level to prevent identity theft and provide assistance to victims, many consumer organizations believe that comprehensive federal legislation is necessary. Several bills (S. 22, S. 153, S. 223, H.R. 220, and H.R. 858) aimed at preventing identity theft and increasing criminal penalties associated with identity theft and related crimes have been introduced during the opening months of the 108th Congress. Generally, these bills mirror proposals from the 107th Congress.

This chapter provides an overview of legislation proposed during the 107th Congress to address the growing problem of identity theft.[1] Much of the legislation from the 107th Congress sought to prevent identity theft through a variety of measures, including placing limitations on the use of social security numbers, requiring the truncation of credit card numbers, and placing additional limitations on access to consumer credit reports. Legislation was also introduced aimed at assisting victims

---

[‡] Excerpted from CRS Report RL31752. Updated February 21, 2003.
[1] For additional information about identity theft and related legislation, see CRS Report RS21083 *Identity Theft and the Fair Credit Reporting Act: An Analysis of TRW v. Andrews and Current Legislation,* and CRS Report 21163, *Remedies Available to Victims of Identity Theft.*

with the oftentimes arduous task of removing information resulting from identity theft from their credit reports, and providing greater criminal penalties for those convicted of identity theft and related crimes. The bills are arranged by chamber and presented in numerical order (Senate Bills: S. 848, S. 1014, S. 1399, S. 1723, S. 1742, S. 2541, S. 3100, House Bills: H.R. 220, H.R. 1478, H.R. 2036, H.R. 3053, H.R. 3368, H.R. 4513, H.R. 4678, H.R. 5424, H.R. 5474, H.R. 5588).

SENATE BILLS

S. 848

The Social Security Number Misuse Prevention Act of 2001, as introduced, would have amended Title 18 of the United States Code to limit the misuse of Social Security numbers and establish criminal penalties for such misuse. The bill would have prohibited the display, sale or purchase of an individual's Social Security number without that individual's "affirmatively expressed consent."[2] The bill would have also prohibited any person from obtaining any individual's Social Security number for purposes of locating or identifying an individual with the intent to physically injure, harm, or use the identity of the individual for any illegal purpose.[3]

Exceptions to the general prohibition included permissible uses under the Social Security Act, the Privacy Act, the Internal Revenue Code, and the Professional Boxing Safety Act of 1996; uses relating to public health, national security or law enforcement; certain business-to-business uses; and required submissions as part of the process for applying for any type of Federal, State, or local government benefit or program.[4] The prohibition would not have applied to Social Security numbers included in certain public records, but agencies would have been required to institute procedures to restrict access to an individual's Social Security number.[5]

The Attorney General was given authority to prescribe rules and regulations necessary to carry out the general prohibition provisions, and is directed to consult with "the Commissioner of Social Security, the Chairman of the Federal Trade Commission, and such other heads of Federal agencies as the Attorney General determines appropriate" to promulgate regulations "to implement and clarify the uses occurring as a result of the interaction between businesses, governments, or businesses and governments."[6] The bill also provided for factors to be considered when promulgating such rules.

---

[2] S. 848, as introduced, Sec. 3.
[3] *Id.*
[4] *Id.*
[5] S. 848, as introduced, Sec. 4.
[6] S. 848, as introduced, Sec. 5.

The bill would have also prohibited the use of Social Security numbers on checks issued by governmental agencies and on driver's licenses, motor vehicle registration documents, or any other document issued to an individual for identification purposes.[7] S. 848 would also prohibit inmate access to Social Security numbers.

Under S. 848, as introduced, a commercial entity would have been prohibited from requiring an individual to provide his or her Social Security number when purchasing a commercial good or service or denying an individual the good or service for refusing to provide the number.[8] The prohibition did not apply with respect to any purpose relating to obtaining a consumer report for any purpose permitted under the Fair Credit Reporting Act; a background check of the individual conducted by a landlord, lessor, employer, voluntary service agency, or other entity as determined by the Attorney General. An individual may have also been required to provide his or her Social Security number for law enforcement purposes; by Federal, State or local law; or if the Social Security number is necessary to verify the identity and to prevent fraud with respect to the specific transaction requested by the consumer and no other form of identification can produce comparable results.[9] These provisions did not prohibit a commercial entity from requiring an individual to provide two forms of identification that do not contain the Social Security number of the individual; or denying an individual a good or service for refusing to provide two forms of such identification.[10]

S. 848, as introduced, also extended civil monetary penalties for misuse of a Social Security number.[11]

S. 848 was referred to the Senate Committee on the Judiciary and reported by Senator Leahy with an amendment in the nature of a substitute on May 16, 2002. The bill was then reported to the Committee on Finance. The Subcommittee on Social Security and Family Policy held hearings on July 11, 2002. No additional action was taken.

As reported, S. 848 included similar provisions relating to prohibitions on the display, sale or purchase of Social Security numbers.[12] However, unlike the introduced version, the bill as reported provided for civil actions in state courts for violations of those prohibitions, and allows an aggrieved individual to recover for actual monetary loss or up to $500 in damages for each violation, whichever is greater.[13] Any such action would have been required to be commenced not later than the earlier of five years after the date on which the alleged violation occurred; or three years after the date on which the alleged violation was or should have been reasonably

---

[7] S. 848, as introduced, Sec. 6.
[8] S. 848, as introduced, Sec. 7.
[9] *Id.*
[10] *Id.*
[11] S. 848, as introduced, Sec. 8.
[12] S. 848, as reported, Sec. 3.
[13] *Id.*

discovered by the aggrieved individual.[14] The bill, as reported, also provided for civil penalties for violations of the prohibitions set forth and criminal sanctions for knowing and willful violations.[15]

The general prohibition would not have applied to Social Security numbers in public records. However, S. 848, as reported, would have required agencies to institute procedures to limit the disclosure of an individual's Social Security number on certain types of records.[16]

S. 1014

The Social Security Number Privacy and Identity Theft Prevention Act of 2001, would have made several amendments to the Social Security Act aimed at enhancing privacy protections for individuals and preventing fraudulent misuse of Social Security numbers. The bill would have prohibited - with limited exceptions - the sale of an individual's Social Security number by any state or federal governmental entity in possession of such number.[17] The display to the general public of an individual's Social Security number would have also been prohibited, as would the display of a Social Security number on any check issued for any payment by any governmental agency.[18] In addition, the appearance of Social Security account numbers on driver's licenses would have been prohibited, as would the display of Social Security numbers on personal identification card or tags provided to state or federal government employees.[19] Access to Social Security numbers by inmates would have also been prohibited, and independent verification of birth records provided by an applicant for a Social Security account number would have been required.[20]

S. 1014 would have also prohibited the sale and display of Social Security numbers in the private sector.[21] The general prohibition would have been subject to certain exceptions. Social Security numbers could have been sold, purchased or displayed to the extent necessary for law enforcement purposes, including the enforcement of a child support obligation; to the extent necessary for national security purposes; to the extent necessary for public health purposes; to the extent necessary in emergency situations; and to the extent necessary for research conducted for the purpose of advancing public knowledge, on the condition that the researcher provide adequate assurances that the privacy of the individual and the individual's number

---

[14] *Id.*
[15] *Id.*
[16] S. 848, as reported, Sec. 4.
[17] S. 1014, Title I, Sec. 101(a).
[18] S. 1014, Title I, Sec. 102, Sec. 103.
[19] S. 1014, Title I, Sec. 104, Sec. 105.
[20] S. 1014, Title I, Sec. 106, Sec. 107.
[21] S. 1014, Title II, Sec. 201.

would have been protected.[22] Individuals would have also been able to consent to the sale, purchase or display of their Social Security numbers. The bill directed the Attorney General to promulgate regulations regarding such restrictions.[23]

S. 1014 would have made refusal to do business without receipt of a Social Security number an unfair or deceptive trade practice under the Federal Trade Commission Act[24] However, situations in which a person was required under federal law to submit an individual's Social Security number in connection with a business transaction would have been exempt.[25]

An amendment to the Fair Credit Reporting Act would have prohibited a credit reporting agency from furnishing an individual's Social Security number unless a full consumer report is being furnished.[26]

With regard to enforcement, S. 1014 would have established new criminal penalties for misuse of a Social Security number, and extends the authority under the Social Security Act to impose civil monetary penalties for misuse of a Social Security number.[27] The bill would have also authorized a court to order a defendant to make restitution to the Social Security Administration.[28]

S. 1014 was referred to the Senate Committee on Finance on June 12, 2001. No additional action was taken.

S. 1399

The Identity Theft Prevention Act of 2001, included several provisions aimed at preventing identity theft. First, the bill would have required credit card issuers to confirm changes of address when a request for an additional card with respect to an existing account is received no more than 30 days after the address change request.[29] Additionally, consumer reporting agencies would have been required to notify requesters of information of potential fraud when the request includes an address for the consumer that differs from the most recent address on file with the consumer reporting agency.[30] The Federal Trade Commission would have had primary enforcement authority, with other agencies responsible for enforcement with respect to entities outside the FTC's jurisdiction.[31]

---

[22] Id.
[23] Id.
[24] S. 1014, Title II, Sec. 202.
[25] Id.
[26] S. 1014, Title II, Sec. 203.
[27] S. 1014, Title III, Sec. 301, Sec. 302.
[28] S. 1014, Title III, Sec. 303.
[29] S.I 399, Sec. 3(a).
[30] Id.
[31] Id.

Under S. 1399, consumer reporting agencies would have also been required to include a fraud alert in a consumer's file, if requested by the consumer.[32] The consumer reporting agency would have been responsible for notifying each person procuring consumer credit information of the existence of a fraud alert in the consumer's file regardless of whether a full credit report, credit score, or summary report is requested.[33]

The bill would have also directed the Federal Trade Commission to promulgate rules requiring each consumer reporting agency to investigate discrepancies between personal or identifying information contained in the file maintained by the agency and the personal identifying information supplied to the agency by the user of the consumer report.[34] The rules promulgated pursuant to S. 1399 would have also been required to include procedures for referral of consumer complaints about identity theft and fraud alerts between and among the consumer reporting agencies and to the Federal Trade Commission.[35]

The truncation of credit card numbers on receipts that are electronically printed would have also been required under S. 1399.[36]

S. 1399 was referred to the Senate Committee on Banking, Housing and Urban Affairs on September 4, 2001. No additional action was taken.

S. 1723

The Protect Victims of Identity Theft Act of 2001, would have amended the Fair Credit Reporting Act's statute of limitations. The amendment proposed under S. 1723 would have allowed suit to be brought "not later than 2 years after the date on which the violation is discovered or should have been discovered by the exercise of reasonable diligence."[37]

S. 1723 was referred to the Senate Committee on Banking, Housing, and Urban Affairs on November 16, 2001. No additional action was taken.

S. 1742

The Restore Your Identity Act of 2001, as introduced, included several provisions aimed at preventing identity theft and aiding victims of identity theft. The bill set forth a mechanism enabling victims of identity theft to receive application and

---

[32] S. 1399, Sec. 3(b).
[33] Id.
[34] S. 1399, Sec. 3(c).
[35] Id.
[36] S. 1399, Sec. 4.
[37] S. 1723, Sec. 2.

Identity Theft: An Overview of Proposed Legislation

transaction information related to the theft from any business entity possessing such information.[38] The bill included provisions for verification of the victim's identity and places limitations on a business' liability with regard to the provision of the requested information.[39] Among the other provisions set forth in the bill was an amendment to the Fair Credit Reporting Act which would have required a consumer reporting agency to "permanently block the reporting of information identified by the consumer in the file of the consumer resulting from the identity theft, so that the information could be reported."[40] Consumer reporting agencies would have had the authority to decline or rescind the request to block information under certain circumstances.[41] Another amendment to the FCRA would have affected the statute of limitations for filing a claim against a credit reporting agency. The proposed amendment would have allowed suit to be filed "not later than two years after the discovery by the individual of the misrepresentation."[42]

The bill also amended the Internet False Identification Act to establish a commission to study coordination between federal, state, and local authorities in enforcing identity theft laws,[43] and provided for enforcement of the provisions set forth in the legislation by state attorneys general and by the Attorney General of the United States.[44]

S. 1742 was referred to the Senate Committee on the Judiciary, and was reported on May 21, 2002, by Senator Leahy with an amendment in the nature of a substitute entitled the Identity Theft Victims Assistance Act of 2002. The amendment was similar to the introduced bill, but some substantive changes were made, including the addition of a provision allowing businesses to establish notification systems to comply with the information sharing provisions discussed above.[45] Additionally, the bill, as reported, provided for enforcement actions by state attorneys general or the Attorney General of the United States for violations of the provisions related to the release of information by business entities.[46]

Substantive changes were also made with regard to the Fair Credit Reporting Act amendments. As reported, S. 1742 included the provisions discussed above related to the blocking of information on a consumer's credit report resulting from an identity theft, but added certain exceptions to the general rule.[47] Additional changes were made to the statute of limitations under the FCRA. S. 1742, as reported, would have

---

[38] S. 1742, as introduced, Sec. 5.
[39] *Id.*
[40] S. 1742, as introduced, Sec. 6.
[41] *Id.*
[42] *Id.*
[43] S. 1742, as introduced, Sec. 7.
[44] S. 1742, as introduced, Sec. 8.
[45] S. 1742, as reported, Sec. 4.
[46] S. 1742, as reported, Sec. 7.
[47] S. 1742, as reported, Sec. 5.

amended the FCRA to allow suit to be brought "not later man 2 years from the date of the defendant's violation of any requirement under this title."[48] Actions by victims of identity theft could have been brought not later than 5 years from the date of the defendant's violation if the victim "has reasonable grounds to 'believe that [he or she] is the victim of an identity theft; and has not materially and willfully misrepresented such a claim."[49]

The Senate passed S. 1742 on November 14, 2002, with an amendment proposed by Senator Reed for Senator Cantwell. As passed, the bill did not include the notification system provision discussed above. Language was included to preclude private rights of action or claims for relief for violations of the provisions related to the release of information by business entities.[50] The bill, as passed, also added to the exceptions related to the blocking of information on a consumer's credit file resulting from an identity theft, and changed the statute of limitations for actions relating to identity theft from 5 years to 4 years.[51]

S. 1742 was referred to the House Committee on the Judiciary and the Committee on Financial Services on November 15, 2002. No additional action was taken by the House of Representatives.

S. 2541

The Identity Theft Penalty Enhancement Act of 2002, would have amended Title 18 of the United States Code to establish penalties for aggravated identity theft and make changes to the existing identity theft provisions of Title 1 S.[52] Under S. 2541, aggravated identity theft would have occurred when a person "knowingly transfers, possesses, or uses, without lawful authority, a means of identification of another person" during and in relation to the commission of certain enumerated felonies.[53] The penalty for aggravated identity theft would have been a term of imprisonment of 2 years in addition to the punishment provided for me original felony committed.[54] The felonies for which a penalty for aggravated identity theft could have been imposed included felonies related to theft *from* employee benefit plans; false impersonation of citizenship; false statements in connection with the acquisition of a firearm; other types of fraud and false statements; mail, bank and wire fraud; fraud relating to passports and visas; violations of the Gramm-Leach-Bliley Act relating to obtaining consumer information under false pretenses; certain violations of the

---

[48] *Id.*
[49] *Id.*
[50] S. 1742, as passed, Sec. 3.
[51] S. 1742, as passed, Sec. 4.
[52] *See* S. 2541, Sec. 3, for amendments to the 18 U.S.C. 1028.
[53] S. 2541, Sec. 2.
[54] *Id.*

Immigration and Nationality Act relating to willfully failing to leave the United States after deportation and creating a counterfeit alien registration card; and certain violations of the Social Security Act.[55]

S. 2541 was referred to the Seriate Committee on the Judiciary. The Subcommittee on Technology, Terrorism, and Government Information held hearings on July 9, 2002. On November 14, 2002, the bill was reported out of Committee favorably and without amendment. No additional action was taken.

S. 3100

The Social Security Number Misuse Prevention Act of 2002, would have amended Title 18 of the United States Code to limit the misuse of Social Security numbers and establish criminal penalties for such misuse. The bill would have prohibited the display, sale or purchase of Social Security numbers without the "affirmatively expressed consent of the individual."[56] Certain exceptions would have applied, including cases where required, authorized, or excepted under any Federal law; for public health purposes; for a national security purpose; for a law enforcement purpose; and under certain circumstances if the display, sale or purchase of the number is for a use occurring as a result of an interaction between businesses, governments, or business and government.[57] The bill provided for limitations on the prohibition with respect to uses permitted under the Gramm-Leach-Bliley Act, the Fair Credit Reporting Act, and with respect to the display, sale or purchase of public records containing Social Security numbers.[58] The Attorney General was given rulemaking authority substantially similar to that provided for in S. 848, as introduced, discussed above.

Additional prohibitions would have applied to the display of the Social Security number, or any derivative of such number, on any check issued for any payment by the Federal, State, or local [social security] agency; on a driver's license, motor vehicle registration or any other document issues for purposes of identification. The bill also prohibited inmate access to Social Security numbers.[59]

In general, S. 3100 precluded a commercial entity from requiring that an individual provide his or her Social Security number when purchasing a consumer good or service, or denying an individual the good or service for failing to provide his or her Social Security number.[60] The preclusion did not apply with respect to any purpose relating to obtaining a consumer report for any purpose permitted under the

---

[55] *Id.*
[56] S. 3100, Sec. 3. These provisions are similar to those in S. 848, as introduced.
[57] *Id.*
[58] S. 3100, Sec. 3 and Sec. 4.
[59] S. 3100, Sec. 6.
[60] S. 3100, Sec. 7.

Fair Credit Reporting Act; a background check of the individual conducted by a landlord, lessor, employer, voluntary service agency, or other entity as determined by the Attorney General. An individual could have also been required to provide his or her Social Security number for law enforcement purposes; by Federal, State or local law; or if the Social Security number is necessary to verify the identity of the consumer to effect, administer, or enforce the specific transaction requested or authorized by the consumer, or to prevent fraud.[61] Violations of these provisions could have been pursued by state attorneys general or by the Attorney General of the United States. The provisions would have expired 6 years after the effective date.[62]

Unrelated to Social Security numbers, an additional section of S. 3100 would have required the truncation of credit card account numbers, prohibiting the printing of more than the last 5 digits of the credit card account number or the expiration date upon any receipt provided to the card holder.[63]

The bill provided for civil monetary penalties, criminal penalties, and civil actions for certain misuses of Social Security numbers.[64]

S. 3100 was placed on the Senate legislative calendar, but no additional action was taken.

HOUSE BILLS

H.R. 220

The **Identity Theft Protection Act of 2001,** would have repealed provisions of the Social Security Act which authorize certain usages of an individual's Social Security number, including, the use of Social Security numbers for general public assistance offered by a state, driver's licenses or motor vehicle registration; and the use of Social Security numbers in the administration of the food stamp program.[65] The bill would have also required all Social Security numbers to be randomly generated and prohibit the Social Security Administration from divulging an individual's account number to any other federal or state governmental entity.[66]

In addition to the provisions related to Social Security numbers, the bill would have prohibited any two agencies or instrumentalities of the federal government from implementing the same identifying number with respect to any individual.[67] The federal government would have also been prohibited from establishing or mandating a

---

[61] *Id.*
[62] *Id.*
[63] S. 3100, Sec. 11.
[64] S. 3100, Sec. 8, Sec. 9, and Sec. 10.
[65] H.R.220,Sec.2.
[66] *Id.*
[67] H.R.220,Sec.4.

uniform standard for identification for an individual; and could not have conditioned the receipt of any federal funding on the adoption, by a state, a state agency, or a political subdivision of a state, of a uniform standard for identification of an individual.[68]

H.R. 220 was referred to the House Committee on Ways and Means and the Committee on Government reform on January 3, 2001, with subsequent referrals to various subcommittees. No additional action was taken.

H.R. 1478

The **Personal Information Privacy Act of 2001,** would have made several amendments to the Fair Credit Reporting Act (FCRA) aimed at protecting a consumer's personal information. The bill would have amended the FCRA to expand the definition of "consumer report" to include "any other identifying information of the consumer, except the name, address, and telephone number of the consumer if listed in a residential telephone directory available in the locality of the consumer."[69] Other amendments to the FCRA would have prohibited the furnishing of consumer credit reports in connection with credit or insurance transactions that were not initiated by the consumer without the consumer's express written authorization and would have required full disclosure to the consumer of what was being authorized and any potential positive and negative effects of such authorization.[70] The sale or transfer of transaction or experience information[71] would have also been prohibited without the express written consent of the consumer.[72]

H.R. 1478 would have also prohibited certain misuses of an individual's Social Security number. The commercial use of an individual's Social Security number would have been prohibited without the written consent of the individual.[73] Refusal to do business with an individual because the individual would not consent to the use of his or her Social Security number would have been treated as an unfair or deceptive act or practice in violation of Section 5 of the Federal Trade Commission Act.[74] The use of an individual's Social Security number as a personal identification number would have also been prohibited without written consent.[75]

---

[68] H.R. 220, Sec. 5.
[69] H.R. 1478, Sec. 2.
[70] H.R. 1478, Sec. 4.
[71] Transaction or experience information is defined as "any information identifying the content or subject of one or more transactions between the consumer and a person doing business with a consumer, including any component part of any transaction, any brand name involved, or any quantity or category of merchandise involved in any party of the transaction." H.R. 1478, Sec. 5.
[72] H.R. 1478, Sec. 5.
[73] H.R. 1478, Sec. 3.
[74] *Id.*
[75] *Id.*

H.R. 1478 was referred to the House Committee on Ways and Means and the Committee on Financial Services on April 24, 2001, with subsequent referrals to the Subcommittee on Financial Institutions and Consumer Credit. No additional action was taken.

H.R. 2036

The **Social Security Number Privacy and Identity Theft Prevention Act of 2001,** was substantially similar to S. 1014 discussed above. H.R. 2036 was referred to the House Committee on Ways and Means, the Committee on Energy and Commerce, and the Committee on Financial Services on May 25, 2001. The bill was subsequently referred to various subcommittees. No additional action was taken.

H.R. 3053

The Identity Theft Prevention Act of 2001, was substantially similar to S. 1399, discussed above. Unlike S. 1399, H.R. 3053 would have required consumer reporting agencies to provide free copies of consumer credit reports on a yearly basis, at the request of the consumer.[76] H.R. 3053 would have also required the Federal Trade Commission to develop a model form and standard procedures to be used by consumers who are victims of identity fraud for contacting and informing creditors and consumer reporting agencies of the fraud.[77]

H.R. 3053 was referred to the House Committee on Financial Services on October 5, 2001, and subsequently to the Subcommittee on Financial Institutions and Consumer Credit. No additional action was taken.

H.R. 3368

The Protect Victims of Identity Theft Act of 2001, was substantially similar to S. 1723 discussed above. The bill would have amended the Fair Credit Reporting Act's statute of limitations. The proposed amendment would have allowed suit to be brought "not later than 2 years after the date on which the violation is discovered or should have been discovered by the exercise of reasonable diligence."[78]

H.R. 3368 was referred to the House Committee on Financial Services on November 28, 2001, and subsequently to the Subcommittee on Financial Institutions

---

[76] H.R. 3053, Sec. 5.
[77] H.R. 3053, Sec. 3(c).
[78] H.R. 3368, Sec. 2.

and Consumer Credit. The bill was also referred to the House Committee on the Judiciary Subcommittee on Courts, the Internet, and Intellectual Property. No additional action was taken.

H.R. 4513

The Social Security Number Protection Act of 2002, included several provisions that were somewhat similar to those in S. 1014 discussed above. H.R. 4513 directed the Federal Trade Commission to promulgate regulations regarding the sale and purchase of Social Security numbers. It would have been unlawful for any person to sell or purchase a Social Security number in a manner that violates a regulation promulgated by the Commission.[79] The Commission was directed to consult with the Commissioner of Social Security, the Department of Justice, and other agencies deemed appropriate to promulgate regulations restricting the sale and purchase of Social Security numbers and any unfair or deceptive acts or practices in connection with the sale and purchase of such.[80] The regulations promulgated were to be no broader than necessary "to provide reasonable assurance that Social Security numbers and Social Security account numbers will not be used to commit or facilitate fraud, deception, or crime; and to prevent an undue risk of bodily, emotional, or financial harm to individuals."[81]

Under H.R. 4513, certain exceptions would have applied to the general restrictions on the sale and purchase of Social Security numbers. The sale and purchase of Social Security numbers would have been permitted under the regulations to the extent necessary for law enforcement and national security purposes; to the extent necessary for public health purposes; to the extent necessary in emergency situations to protect the health or safety of one or more individuals; and to the extent necessary for research conducted for the purpose of advancing public knowledge, on the condition that the researcher provided adequate assurances that certain measures would have been employed to protect the privacy of the individual and the confidentiality of the individual's Social Security number.[82] An individual could have also consented to the sale or purchase of his or her Social Security number.[83]

Violations of the regulations promulgated pursuant to H.R. 4513 would have been enforced by the Federal Trade Commission and treated as an unfair or deceptive act or practice.[84] State attorneys general would have also had authority to bring actions

---

[79] H.R.4513, Sec.4(a).
[80] H.R.4513, Sec.4(b)(1).
[81] H.R.4513, Sec.4(b)(2).
[82] H.R.4513, Sec.4(b)(3).
[83] *Id.*
[84] H.R.4513, Sec.4(d).

on behalf of the residents of their states.[85] The Attorney General of the United States would have also had some enforcement authority.[86]

H.R. 4513 was referred to the House Committee on Energy and Commerce and the Committee on Ways and Means on April 18, 2002. No additional action was taken.

H.R. 4678

The Consumer Privacy Protection Act of 2002, included provisions related to both privacy protection and identity theft. Title I of H.R. 4678 specifically addressed privacy with regard to consumer information gathered and used by data collection organizations, and included provisions related to privacy statements, opt-out opportunities for consumers, information security obligations, and self-regulatory programs for data collection organizations. Title II of the bill specifically addressed identity theft prevention and remedies. These provisions will be discussed in detail below.

Title II of H.R. 4678 directed the Federal Trade Commission to take specific actions to assist victims of identity theft. The Commission was directed to take such action as necessary to permit (including by electronic means) consumers that have a reasonable belief that they are a victims of identity theft to enter required consumer information into the commission-developed "Identity Theft Affidavit," and to submit completed forms and other supplemental information to the Commission and other entities.[87] The Commission would have also been required to "take such action as necessary to solicit the acceptance and acknowledgment of standardized Identity Theft Affidavit by entities that receive disputes regarding the unauthorized use of accounts of such entities from consumers that have reason to believe that they are a victim of identity theft."[88] Additionally, the Commission would have required such entities to conduct any necessary investigation and decide an outcome of a claim from a consumer within 90 days from the date on which all necessary information has been submitted.[89]

Under H.R. 4678, the Federal Trade Commission would have also been required to make improvements to the Identity Theft Clearinghouse which would allow consumers to submit identity theft information to appropriate entities via the Clearinghouse.[90] The Commission would have also been required to obtain identity theft data from public and private entities that receive and process complaints from

---

[85] H.R.4513, Sec.4(e).
[86] *Id.*
[87] H.R. 4678, Sec. 201.
[88] H.R. 4678, Sec. 202.
[89] H.R. 4678, Sec. 203.
[90] H.R. 4678, Sec. 204.

consumers and include such information in the Identity Theft Clearinghouse database.[91]

In an effort to prevent identity theft, H.R. 4678 directed the Commission to require "appropriate entities to take reasonable steps to verify the accuracy of a consumer's address, including by confirming a consumer's change of address by sending a confirmation of such change to the old and new address of the consumer."[92]

H.R. 4678 was referred to the House Committee on Energy and Commerce Subcommittee on Commerce, Trade and Consumer Protection. Subcommittee hearings were held on September 24, 2002, but not additional action was taken.[93]

H.R. 5424

The **Identity Theft Victims Assistance Act of 2002,** appeared to be substantially similar to S. 1742, as reported, discussed above. H.R. 5424 was referred to the House Committee on the Judiciary and the Committee on Financial Services on September 19, 2002, and subsequently to the Subcommittee on Crime, Terrorism and Homeland Security and the Subcommittee on Financial Institutions and Consumer Credit. No additional action was taken.

H.R. 5474

The **Identity Theft Consumer Notification Act,** would have amended the Gramm-Leach-Bliley Act to further protect consumers whose identities are stolen from their financial institutions. Under H.R. 5474, a financial institution would have been required to promptly notify a consumer if his or her personal information had been compromised in any way by an employee of the financial institution or through any unauthorized entry into the records of the institution.[94] In the event of such compromise, the financial institution would have been obligated to notify the consumer of the compromise and any misuse of the information; to provide assistance to the consumer to remedy any such compromise; to reimburse the consumer for any losses the consumer incurred as a result of the compromise, including any fees for obtaining, investigating, and correcting a consumer report; and to provide information concerning the manner in which the consumer can obtain such assistance.[95] Financial institutions would have been able to delay notification at the request of a law

---

[91] H.R. 4678, Sec. 205.
[92] H.R. 4678, Sec. 206.
[93] Title III of the bill includes provisions related to international privacy laws which were referred to the House Committee on International Relations.
[94] H.R. 5474, Sec. 2.
[95] *Id.*

enforcement agency investigating the violation that led to the compromise of the consumer's information.

The bill would have also amended the Fair Credit Reporting Act's statute of limitations to allow an action to be brought "not later than 2 years after the date on which the violation is discovered or should have been discovered by the exercise of reasonable diligence."[96]

H.R. 5474 was referred to the House Committee on Financial Services Subcommittee on Financial Institutions and Consumer Credit on October 7, 2002. No additional action was taken.

H.R. 5588. The Identity Theft Penalty Enhancement Act of 2002, was substantially similar to S. 2541 discussed above. H.R. 5588 was referred to the House Committee on the Judiciary Subcommittee on Crime, Terrorism, and Homeland Security on November 12, 2002. No additional action was taken.

---

[96] H.R. 5474, Sec. 3.

Chapter 2

IDENTITY THEFT: PREVALENCE AND COST APPEAR TO BE GROWING[*]

Richard M. Stana

This chapter reviews and compiles the latest statistics on the incidence and societal cost of identity theft. Generally, as noted in our May 1998 report,[1] identify theft or identity fraud involves "stealing" another person's personal identifying information—such as Social Security number (SSN), date of birth, and mother's maiden name—and then using the information to fraudulently establish credit, run up debt, or take over existing financial accounts. Later that year, Congress passed legislation—the Identity Theft and Assumption Deterrence Act of 1998 (the Identity Theft Act)[2]—which separately made identity theft a specific federal crime and recognized that victims include individuals, as well as financial institutions and other business entities. Also, since 1998, most states have enacted laws that criminalize identity theft.

Specifically, this chapter provides information on

- the extent or prevalence of identity theft;

---

[*] Excerptedf from General Accounting Office (GAO) Report GAO-02-363.
[1] U.S. General Accounting Office, *Identity Fraud: Information on Prevalence, Cost, and Internet Impact is Limited,* GAO/GGD-98-100BR (Washington, D.C.: May 1, 1998).
[2] Public Law 105-318 (1998). The relevant section of this legislation is codified at 18 U.S.C. § 1028(a)(7) ("fraud and related activity in connection with identification documents and information").

- the cost of identity theft to the financial services industry,[3] including direct fraud losses, staffing of fraud departments, and effect on consumer confidence in online commerce;
- the cost of identity theft to victims, including victim productivity losses, out-of-pocket expenses, and cost of being denied credit; and
- the cost of identity theft to the federal criminal justice system.

To address these topics, we interviewed responsible officials and reviewed documentation obtained from relevant federal agencies—the Department of Justice and its components, including the Executive Office for U.S. Attorneys (EOUSA) and the Federal Bureau of Investigation (FBI); Department of the Treasury and its components, including the Secret Service and the Internal Revenue Service (IRS); the Social Security Administration's (SSA) Office of the Inspector General (OIG); the Postal Inspection Service; and the Federal Trade Commission (FTC). Also, we contacted representatives of the three national consumer reporting agencies and two payment card associations (MasterCard and Visa). Furthermore, at our request and with the consent of the victims, FTC provided us with the names and telephone numbers of a small cross section of victims (10 total) to interview. According to FTC staff, the sample of 10 victims was selected to illustrate a range in the extent and variety of the identity theft activities reported by victims. The experiences of these 10 victims are not statistically representative of all victims. We conducted our work from March 2001 to January 2002 in accordance with generally accepted government auditing standards.

RESULTS

No single hotline or database captures the universe of identity theft victims. Some individuals do not even know that they have been victimized until months after the fact, and some known victims may choose not to report to the police, credit bureaus, or established hotlines. Thus, it is difficult to fully or accurately quantify the prevalence of identity theft. Some of the often-quoted estimates of prevalence range from one-quarter to three-quarters of a million victims annually. Usually, these estimates are based on limited hotline reporting or other available data, in combination with various assumptions regarding, for example, the number of victims who do not contact credit bureaus, the FTC, the SSA/OIG, or other authorities. Generally

---

[3] Generally, regarding the financial services industry, the scope of our work focused primarily on obtaining information from banks, two payment card associations (MasterCard and Visa), and national consumer reporting agencies (commonly referred to as "credit bureaus"). We did not obtain information about losses involving other generalpurpose cards (American Express, Diners Club, and Discover) nor losses involving merchant-specific cards issued by retail stores.

speaking, the higher the estimate of identity theft prevalence, the greater the (1) number of victims who are assumed not to report the crime and (2) number of hotline callers who are assumed to be victims rather than "preventative" callers. We found no information to gauge the extent to which these assumptions are valid. Additionally, there are no readily available statistics on the number of victims who may have contacted their banks or credit card issuers only and not the credit bureaus or other hotlines.

Nevertheless, although not specifically or comprehensively quantifiable, the prevalence and cost of identity theft seem to be increasing, according to the available data we reviewed and many officials of the public and private sector entities we contacted. The following presents summary information for each of the topics that we addressed. More detailed information is presented in appendixes II through V, respectively.

Prevalence of Identity Theft

As we reported in 1998, there are no comprehensive statistics on the prevalence of identity theft. Similarly, during our current review, various officials noted that precise, statistical measurement of identity theft trends is difficult due to a number of factors. Generally, federal law enforcement agencies do not have information systems that facilitate specific tracking of identity theft cases. For example, while the amendments made by the Identity Theft Act are included as subsection (a)(7) of section 1028, Title 18 of the U.S. Code, EOUSA does not have comprehensive statistics on offenses charged specifically under that subsection. EOUSA officials explained that, except for certain firearms statutes, docketing staff are asked to record cases under only the U.S. Code section, not the subsection or the sub-subsection. Also, the FBI and the Secret Service noted that identity theft is not typically a stand-alone crime; rather, identity theft is almost always a component of one or more white-collar or financial crimes, such as bank fraud, credit card or access device fraud, or the use of counterfeit financial instruments.

Nonetheless, while recognizing measurement difficulties, a number of data sources can be used as proxies or indicators for gauging the prevalence of such crime. These sources can include consumer complaints and hotline allegations, as well as law enforcement investigations and prosecutions of identity theft-related crimes such as bank fraud and credit card fraud. Each of these various sources or measures seems to indicate that the prevalence of identity theft is growing:

Consumer Reporting Agency Data

Generally, in the view of consumer reporting agency officials, the most reliable indicator of the incidence of identity theft is the number of 7-year fraud alerts placed on consumer credit files. Generally, fraud alerts constitute a warning that someone may be using the consumer's personal information to fraudulently obtain credit. Thus, a purpose of the alert is to advise credit grantors to conduct additional identity verification or contact the consumer directly before granting credit. One of the three consumer reporting agencies estimated that its 7-year fraud alerts involving identity theft increased 36 percent over 2 recent years—from about 65,600 in 1999 to 89,000 in 2000.[4] A second agency reported that its 7-year fraud alerts increased about 53 percent in recent comparative 12-month periods; that is, the number increased from 19,347 during one 12-month period (July 1999 through June 2000) to 29,593 during the more recent period (July 2000 through June 2001). The third agency reported about 92,000 fraud alerts[5] for 2000 but was unable to provide information for any earlier year.[6] Also, due largely to increased public awareness about identity theft, the number of inquiries received by the fraud units of consumer reporting agencies is at an all-time high. However, an industry official opined that the number of inquiries is not a reasonable measure of the incidence of identity theft because virtually all individuals whose wallet or purse is lost or stolen will now call the consumer reporting agencies as a precautionary measure.

FTC data

From its establishment in November 1999 through September 2001, FTC's Identity Theft Data Clearinghouse received a total of 94,100 complaints from victims, including 16,784 complaints transferred to the FTC from the SSA/OIG. In the first month of operation, the Clearinghouse answered an average of 445 calls per week. By March 2001, the average number of calls answered had increased to over 2,000 per week. In December 2001, the weekly average was about 3,000 answered calls. However, FTC officials noted that identity theft-related statistics may, in part, reflect enhanced consumer awareness and reporting.

SSA/OIG data

SSA/OIG has reported a substantial increase in call-ins of identity theft-related allegations to its Fraud Hotline in recent years. Allegations involving SSN misuse, for example, increased more than fivefold, from about 11,000 in fiscal year 1998 to about 65,000 in fiscal year 2001. To some extent, the increased number of allegations may

---

[4] These estimates are approximations based on the judgment and experience of agency officials.
[5] The duration of this agency's fraud alerts can vary from 2 to 7 years, at the discretion of the individual consumer.
[6] An aggregate figure—totaling the number of fraud alerts reported by the three consumer reporting agencies—may be misleading, given the likelihood that many consumers may have contacted more than one agency. During our review, we noted that various Web sites—including those of two of the three national consumer reporting agencies, as well as the FTC's Web site—advise individuals who believe they are the victims of identity theft or fraud to contact all three national consumer reporting agencies.

be due to additional Fraud Hotline staffing, which increased from 11 to over 50 personnel during this period. However, SSA/OIG officials attributed the trend in allegations partly to a greater incidence of identity theft. Also, irrespective of staffing levels, SSA/OIG data indicate that about 81 percent of all allegations of SSN misuse relate directly to identity theft.

Federal Law Enforcement Data

Generally, although federal law enforcement agencies do not have information systems that facilitate specific tracking of identity theft cases, the agencies provided us case statistics for identity theft-related crimes. Regarding bank fraud, for instance, the FBI reported that its arrests increased from 579 in 1998 to 645 in 2000—and was even higher (691) in 1999. The Secret Service reported that, for recent years, it has redirected its identity theft-related efforts to focus on high-dollar, community-impact cases. Thus, even though the total number of identity theft-related cases closed by the Secret Service decreased from 8,498 in fiscal year 1998 to 7,071 in 2000, the amount of fraud losses prevented in these cases increased from a reported average of $73,382 in 1998 to an average of $217,696 in 2000.[7] The Postal Inspection Service, in its fiscal year 2000 annual report, noted that identity theft is a growing trend and that the agency's investigations of such crime had "increased by 67 percent since last year."

Cost of Identity Theft to the Financial Services Industry

We found no comprehensive estimates of the cost of identity theft to the financial services industry. Some data on identity theft-related losses—such as direct fraud losses reported by the American Bankers Association (ABA) and payment card associations—indicated increasing costs. Other data, such as staffing of the fraud departments of banks and consumer reporting agencies, presented a mixed and/or incomplete picture. For example, one consumer reporting agency reported that staffing of its fraud department had doubled in recent years, whereas another agency reported relatively constant staffing levels. Furthermore, despite concerns about security and privacy, the use of e-commerce has grown steadily in recent years. Such growth may indicate greater consumer confidence but may also have resulted from an increase in the number of people who have access to Internet technology.

Regarding direct fraud losses, in its year 2000 bank industry survey on check fraud, the ABA reported that total check fraud-related losses against commercial bank accounts—considering both actual losses ($679 million) and loss avoidance ($1.5 billion)—reached an estimated $2.2 billion in 1999, which was twice the amount in

---

[7] In compiling case statistics, the Secret Service defined "identity theft" as any case related to the investigation of false, fraudulent, or counterfeit identification; stolen, counterfeit, or altered checks or Treasury securities; stolen, altered, or counterfeit credit cards; or financial institution fraud.

1997.[8] Regarding actual losses, the report noted that the 1999 figure ($679 million) was up almost 33 percent from the 1997 estimate ($512 million). However, not all check fraud-related losses were attributed to identity theft, which the ABA defined as account takeovers (or true name fraud). Rather, the ABA reported that, of the total check fraud-related losses in 1999, the percentages attributable to identity theft ranged from 56 percent for community banks (assets under $500 million) to 5 percent for superregional/money center banks (assets of $50 billion or more), and the average for all banks was 29 percent.

The two major payment card associations, MasterCard and Visa, use very similar (although not identical) definitions regarding which categories of fraud constitute identity theft. Generally, the associations consider identity theft to consist of two fraud categories—account takeovers and fraudulent applications.[9] Based on these two categories, the associations' aggregated identity theft-related losses from domestic (U.S. operations) rose from $79.9 million in 1996 to $114.3 million in 2000, an increase of about 43 percent. The associations' definitions of identity theft-related fraud are relatively narrow, in the view of law enforcement, which considers identity theft as encompassing virtually all categories of payment card fraud. Under this broader definition, the associations' total fraud losses from domestic operations rose from about $700 million in 1996 to about $1.0 billion in 2000, an increase of about 45 percent. However, according to the associations, the annual total fraud losses represented about 1/10th of 1 percent or less of U.S. member banks' annual sales volume during 1996 through 2000. Generally, the fraud losses are borne by the respective financial institution that issued the payment card.

To reiterate, regarding direct fraud losses involving payment cards, we contacted MasterCard and Visa only. We did not obtain information about losses involving other general-purpose cards (American Express, Diners Club, and Discover), which account for about 25 percent of the market. Also, we did not obtain information about losses involving merchant-specific cards issued by retail stores. Furthermore, we did not obtain information from various other entities, such as insurance companies and securities firms, which may incur identity theft-related costs.

Regarding staffing and cost of fraud departments, in its year 2000 bank industry survey on check fraud, the ABA reported that the amount of resources that banks devoted to check fraud prevention, detection, investigation, and prosecution varied according to bank size. For check fraud-related operating expenses (not including actual losses) in 1999, the ABA reported that over two-thirds of the 446 community

---

[8] ABA, *Deposit Account Fraud Survey Report 2000*. The ABA defined "loss avoidance" as the amount of losses avoided as a result of the banks' prevention systems and procedures. Because the overall response rate by banks to the survey was 11 percent, the ABA's data should be interpreted with caution.

[9] Other fraud categories that the associations do not consider to be identity theft-related include, for example, lost and stolen cards, never-received cards, counterfeit cards, and mail order/telephone order fraud.

banks that responded to the survey each spent less than $10,000, and about one-fourth of the 11 responding superregional/money center banks each spent $10 million or more for such expenses.

One national consumer reporting agency told us that staffing of its Fraud Victim Assistance Department doubled in recent years, increasing from 50 individuals in 1997 to 103 in 2001. The total cost of the department was reported to be $4.3 million for 2000. Although not as specific, a second agency reported that the cost of its fraud assistance staffing was "several million dollars." And, the third consumer reporting agency said that the number of fraud operators in its Consumer Services Center had increased in the 1990's but has remained relatively constant at about 30 to 50 individuals since 1997.

Regarding consumer confidence in online commerce, despite concerns about security and privacy, the use of e-commerce by consumers has steadily grown. For example, in the year 2000 holiday season, consumers spent an estimated $10.8 billion online, which represented more than a 50-percent increase over the $7 billion spent during the 1999 holiday season. Furthermore, in 1995, only one bank had a Web site capable of processing financial transactions but, by 2000, a total of 1,850 banks and thrifts had Web sites capable of processing financial transactions.[10]

The growth in e-commerce could indicate greater consumer confidence but could also result from the increasing number of people who have access to and are becoming familiar with Internet technology. According to an October 2000 Department of Commerce report, Internet users comprised about 44 percent (approximately 116 million people) of the U.S. population in August 2000. This was an increase of about 38 percent from 20 months prior.[11] According to Commerce's report, the fastest growing online activity among Internet users was online shopping and bill payment, which grew at a rate of 52 percent in 20 months.

Cost of Identity Theft to Victims

Identity theft can cause substantial harm to the lives of individual citizens—potentially severe emotional or other nonmonetary harm, as well as economic harm. Even though financial institutions may not hold victims liable for fraudulent debts, victims nonetheless often feel "personally violated" and have reported spending significant amounts of time trying to resolve the problems caused by identity theft—

---

[10] Federal Deposit Insurance Corporation, *Evolving Financial Products, Services, and Delivery Systems* (Feb. 14, 2001).

[11] Department of Commerce, *Falling Through The Net: Toward Digital Inclusion* (Oct. 2000). This report was the fourth in a series of studies issued by Commerce on the technological growth of U.S. households and individuals.

problems such as bounced checks, loan denials, credit card application rejections, and debt collection harassment.

For the 23-month period from its establishment in November 1999 through September 2001, the FTC Identity Theft Data Clearinghouse received 94,100 complaints from victims, including complaint data contributed by SSA/OIG. The leading types of nonmonetary harm cited by consumers were "denied credit or other financial services" (mentioned in over 7,000 complaints) and "time lost to resolve problems" (mentioned in about 3,500 complaints). Also, in nearly 1,300 complaints, identity theft victims alleged that they had been subjected to "criminal investigation, arrest, or conviction." Regarding monetary harm, FTC Clearinghouse data for the 23-month period indicated that 2,633 victims reported dollar amounts as having been lost or paid as out-of-pocket expenses as a result of identity theft. Of these 2,633 complaints, 207 each alleged losses above $5,000; another 203 each alleged losses above $10,000.

From its database of identity theft victims, after obtaining the individuals' consent, FTC provided us the names and telephone numbers of 10 victims, whom we contacted to obtain an understanding of their experiences. In addition to the types of harm mentioned above, several of the victims expressed feelings of "invaded privacy" and "continuing trauma." In particular, such "lack of closure" was cited when elements of the crime involved more than one jurisdiction and/or if the victim had no awareness of any arrest being made. For instance, some victims reported being able to file a police report in their state of residence but were unable to do so in other states where the perpetrators committed fraudulent activities using the stolen identities. Only 2 of the 10 victims told us they were aware that the perpetrator had been arrested.

In a May 2000 report, two nonprofit advocacy entities—the California Public Interest Research Group (CALPIRG) and the Privacy Rights Clearinghouse—presented findings based on a survey (conducted in the spring of 2000) of 66 identity theft victims who had contacted these organizations.[12] According to the report, the victims spent 175 hours, on average, actively trying to resolve their identity theft-related problems. Also, not counting legal fees, most victims estimated spending $100 for out-of-pocket costs. The May 2000 report stated that these findings may not be representative of the plight of all victims. Rather, the report noted that the findings should be viewed as "preliminary and representative only of those victims who have contacted our organizations for further assistance (other victims may have had simpler cases resolved with only a few calls and felt no need to make further inquiries)."

---

[12] CALPIRG (Sacramento, Cal.) and Privacy Rights Clearinghouse (San Diego, Cal.), "Nowhere to Turn: Victims Speak Out on Identity Theft" (May 2000).

Federal Criminal Justice System Costs

Regarding identity theft and any other type of crime, the federal criminal justice system incurs costs associated with investigations, prosecutions, incarceration, and community supervision.[13] Generally, we found that federal agencies do not separately maintain statistics on the person hours, portions of salary, or other distinct costs that are specifically attributable to cases involving identity theft. As an alternative, some of the agencies provided us with average cost estimates based, for example, on work-year counts for white-collar crime cases—a category that covers financial crimes, including identity theft.

In response to our request, the FBI estimated that the average cost of an investigative matter handled by the agency's white-collar crime program was approximately $20,000 during fiscal years 1998 to 2000, based on budget and workload data for the 3 years. However, an FBI official cautioned that the average cost figure has no practical significance because it does not capture the wide variance in the scope and costs of white-collar crime investigations. Also, the official cautioned that—while identity theft is frequently an element of bank fraud, wire fraud, and other types of white-collar or financial crimes—some cases (including some high-cost cases) do not involve elements of identity theft.

Similarly, Secret Service officials—in responding to our request for an estimate of the average cost of investigating financial crimes that included identity theft as a component—said that cases vary so much in their makeup that to put a figure on average cost is not meaningful. Nonetheless, the agency's Management and Organization Division made its "best estimate of the average cost" of a financial crimes investigation conducted by the Secret Service in fiscal year 2001. The resulting estimate was approximately $15,000. Secret Service officials noted that this estimate was for a financial crimes investigation and not specifically for an identity theft investigation. Also, the officials emphasized that, in the absence of specific guidelines establishing a standard methodology, average-cost figures provide no basis for making interagency comparisons.

SSA/OIG officials responded that the agency's information systems do not record time spent by function to permit making an accurate estimate of what it costs the OIG to investigate cases of SSN misuse. Also, in commenting on a draft of this chapter, the Commissioner, SSA, said that SSA/OIG's priorities are appropriately targeted to SSA's program integrity areas and business processes rather than specifically on identity theft, which is investigated by many different federal and state agencies.

---

[13] As agreed with the requesters, this section of our report focuses on costs of identity theft to the federal government only and not to state or local governmental entities; although, since 1998, most states have enacted laws that criminalize identity theft.

Regarding prosecutions, in fiscal year 2000, federal prosecutors dealt with approximately 13,700 white-collar crime cases, at an estimated average cost of about $11,400 per case, according to EOUSA. The total cases included those that were closed in the year, those that were opened in the year, and those that were still pending at year-end. EOUSA noted that the $11,400 figure was an estimate and that the actual cost could be higher or lower.

According to Bureau of Prisons (BOP) officials, federal offenders convicted of white-collar crimes generally are incarcerated in minimum-security facilities. For fiscal year 2000, the officials said that the cost of operating such facilities averaged about $17,400 per inmate.

After being released from BOP custody, offenders are typically supervised in the community by federal probation officers for a period of 3 to 5 years. For fiscal year 2000, according to the Administrative Office of the United States Courts, the cost of community supervision averaged about $2,900 per offender—which is an average for "regular supervision" without special conditions, such as community service, electronic monitoring, or substance abuse treatment.

CONCLUDING OBSERVATIONS

Since our May 1998 report, various actions—particularly passage of federal and state statutes—have been taken to address identity theft. The federal statute,[14] enacted in October 1998, made identity theft a separate crime against the person whose identity was stolen, broadened the scope of the offense to include the misuse of information as well as documents, and provided punishment—generally, a fine or imprisonment for up to 15 years or both. Under U.S. Sentencing Commission guidelines—even if (1) there is no monetary loss and (2) the perpetrator has no prior criminal convictions—a sentence as high as 10 to 16 months incarceration can be imposed. Regarding state statutes, at the time of our 1998 report, very few states had specific laws to address identity theft. Now, less than 4 years later, a large majority of states have enacted identity theft statutes.

In short, federal and state legislation indicate that identity theft has been widely recognized as a serious crime across the nation. As such, a current focus for policymakers and criminal justice administrators is to ensure that relevant legislation is effectively enforced. Given the frequently cross-jurisdictional nature of identity theft crime, enforcement of the relevant federal and state laws presents various challenges, particularly regarding coordination of efforts. Although we have not evaluated them, initiatives designed to address these challenges include the following:

---

[14] Public Law 105-318 (1998).

- After enactment of the 1998 Identity Theft Act, the Attorney General's Council on White Collar Crime established a Subcommittee on Identity Theft. Purposes of the Subcommittee are to foster coordination of investigative and prosecutorial strategies and promote consumer education programs. Subcommittee leadership is vested in the Fraud Section of the Department of Justice's Criminal Division, and membership includes representatives from various Justice, Treasury, and State Department components; SSA/OIG; the FTC; federal regulatory agencies, such as the Office of the Comptroller of the Currency and the Federal Deposit Insurance Corporation; and professional organizations, such as the International Association of Chiefs of Police (IACP), the National Association of Attorneys General, and the National District Attorneys Association.

- Various identity theft task forces, with multiagency participation (including state and local law enforcement), have been established to investigate and prosecute cases. Such task forces enable law enforcement to more effectively pursue cases that have multi-jurisdictional elements, such as fraudulent schemes that involve illegal activities in multiple counties or states. At the time of our review, the Secret Service was the lead agency in 37 task forces across the country that were primarily targeting financial and electronic crimes, many of which may include identity theft-related elements.

- Also, under the 1998 Identity Theft Act, the FTC established a toll-free number for victims to call and is compiling complaint information in a national Identity Theft Data Clearinghouse. FTC's Consumer Sentinel Network makes this information available to federal, state, and local law enforcement. According to FTC staff, use of the Consumer Sentinel Network enables law enforcement to coordinate efforts and to pinpoint high-impact or other significant episodes of identity theft.

Furthermore, there is general agreement that, in addition to investigating and prosecuting perpetrators, a multipronged approach to combating identity theft must include prevention efforts, such as limiting access to personal information. In this regard, federal law enacted in 1999, the Gramm-Leach-Bliley Act,[15] directed financial institutions—banks, savings associations, credit unions, broker-dealers, investment companies, investment advisers, and insurance companies—to have policies, procedures, and controls in place to prevent the unauthorized disclosure of customer financial information and to deter fraudulent access to such information. Prevention efforts by financial institutions are particularly important, given FTC data showing

---

[15] Public Law 106-102 (1999).

that a large majority of consumer complaints regarding identity theft involve financial services—new credit card accounts opened, existing credit card accounts used, new deposit accounts opened, and newly obtained loans.

Finally, given indications that the prevalence and cost of identity theft have increased in recent years, most observers agree that such crime certainly warrants continued attention from law enforcement, industry, and consumers.[16] Also, due partly to the growth of the Internet and other communications technologies, there is general consensus that the opportunities for identity theft are not likely to decline.

APPENDIX I: PREVALENCE OF IDENTITY THEFT

This appendix presents information about the prevalence of identity theft, that is, the extent or incidence of such theft. Some individuals do not even know that they have been victimized until months after the fact, and some known victims may choose not to report to the police, credit bureaus, or established hotlines. Thus, it is difficult to fully or accurately quantify the prevalence of identity theft. Some of the often-quoted estimates of prevalence range from one-quarter to three-quarters of a million victims annually. Usually, these estimates are based on limited hotline reporting or other available data, in combination with various assumptions regarding, for example, the number of victims who do not contact credit bureaus, the FTC, the SSA/OIG, or other authorities. Generally speaking, the higher the estimate of identity theft prevalence, the greater the (1) number of victims who are assumed not to report the crime and (2) number of hotline callers who are assumed to be victims rather than "preventative" callers. We found no information to gauge the extent to which these assumptions are valid. Additionally, there are no readily available statistics on the number of victims who may have contacted their banks or credit card issuers only and not the credit bureaus or other hotlines.

As we reported in 1998, there are no comprehensive statistics on the prevalence of identity theft.[17] Similarly, during our current review, various officials noted that precise, statistical measurement of identity theft trends is difficult due to a number of factors. The Secret Service noted, for instance, that identity theft is not typically a stand-alone crime; rather, identity theft is almost always a component of one or more crimes, such as bank fraud, credit card or access device fraud, or the use of counterfeit financial instruments. Nonetheless, while recognizing measurement difficulties, a number of data sources can be used as proxies or indicators for gauging the prevalence of such crime. These sources can include consumer complaints and hotline allegations as well as law enforcement investigations and prosecutions. Each of these

---

[16] Appendix VI lists contact points for reporting identity theft and seeking assistance.
[17] U.S. General Accounting Office, *Identity Fraud: Information on Prevalence, Cost, and Internet Impact is Limited*, GAO/GGD-98-100BR (Washington, D.C.: May 1, 1998).

various sources or measures seems to indicate that the prevalence of identity theft is growing. This appendix summarizes statistical and related information we obtained from

- the three national consumer reporting agencies (CRAs) that have call-in centers for reporting identity fraud or theft;
- the Federal Trade Commission (FTC), which maintains a database of complaints concerning identity theft;
- the Social Security Administration's Office of the Inspector General (SSA/OIG), which operates a hotline to receive allegations of SSN misuse and program fraud; and
- federal law enforcement agencies—Department of Justice components, Department of the Treasury components, and the Postal Inspection Service—responsible for investigating and prosecuting identity theft-related cases.

National Consumer Reporting Agencies

Statistics provided to us by the three national CRAs included the number and types of fraud alerts placed on consumers' credit files, as well as the number of inquiries (call volume) received by the fraud units of the CRAs. Generally, fraud alerts constitute a warning that someone may be using the consumer's personal information to fraudulently obtain credit. Thus, a purpose of the alert is to advise credit grantors to conduct additional identity verification or contact the consumer directly before granting credit.

Due largely to increased public awareness about identity fraud, the number of inquiries received by the fraud units of CRAs is at an all-time high. For instance, a senior official of one CRA told us that his agency's fraud unit experienced an 84-percent increase in inquires from 1998 to 2000. Now, the CRA official opined, virtually all individuals whose wallet or purse is lost or stolen will call a CRA as a precautionary measure.

According to industry officials, individuals who suspect that they have been the victims of fraud will generally contact all three national CRAs rather than just one or two.[18] Thus, industry officials told us that there probably is a high degree of overlap in each CRA's respective fraud statistics. Also, the officials said that any large variations

---

[18] During our review, we noted that various Web sites—including those of two of the three national CRAs, as well as the FTC's Web site—advise individuals who believe they are the victims of identity theft or fraud to contact all three national CRAs.

in reported statistics among the national CRAs are generally the result of different methods for classifying fraud-related inquiries.

In obtaining statistics from the three national CRAs, we agreed to report the information in a manner not specifically identifiable to the respective agency. Thus, in the following sections, we refer to the three sources as "Agency A," "Agency B," and "Agency C."

Agency A: Number of Files with Fraud Alerts

Agency A officials provided us with trend statistics on the number of individual credit files that had a 7-year fraud alert posted by the agency's fraud victim assistance division. Regarding the total number of consumers helped by this division, the officials said that the number of fraud alert postings is a better indicator than the number of consumer contacts with the division. The officials explained that:

- The number of consumer contacts may include some double counting. For instance, the same consumer may call or write the fraud victim assistance division more than once.

- In contrast, for any given time period, the agency will post a fraud alert only once to an individual consumer's file. Thus, there is no double counting in these statistics.

Furthermore, the officials noted that, based on the agency's best judgment and years of experience with 7-year fraud alert postings, the reasons for such postings can be grouped into three categories.

- About 50 percent of the postings are based on preventative calls from consumers rather than actual or verified instances of fraud. Generally, these consumers request a fraud alert from the standpoint of being "safe rather than sorry"—a preventative approach.

- Another 25 percent of the postings are based on credit card account takeovers. The agency does not define or consider these postings as involving "identity fraud."

- The remaining 25 percent of the postings are based on identity fraud. Most of these instances involve fraudulent credit card applications.

Identity Theft: Prevalence and Cost Appear to be Growing   31

Table 1: Number of Files with Fraud
Alerts Posted (Agency A), 1995 through 2000

Year fraud alert posted[a]	Expiration year of fraud alert	Number of files with fraud alert[b]	Reason for fraud alert: preventative (50 percent)	Reason for fraud alert: account takeover (25 percent)	Reason for fraud alert: identity fraud (25 percent)
1995	2002	111,287	55,600	27,800	27,800
1996	2003	172,319	86,200	43,100	43,100
1997	2004	168,992	84,500	42,200	42,200
1998	2005	191,321	95,700	47,800	47,800
1999	2006	262,410	131,200	65,600	65,600
2000	2007	356,001	178,000	89,000	89,000

Note: Agency A ran a special scan on the agency's national database to produce counts of the number of individual credit files that had a 7-year fraud alert posted. To array the count data, the agency sorted the counts by year of the alert's expiration. According to agency officials, most fraud alerts are posted for 7 years, unless the consumer requests a shorter period.

[a] We calculated these dates by subtracting 7 years from the expiration year shown in the next column.

[b] As noted in the table, Agency A officials determined these counts based on a special scan of the agency's national database. The agency used these counts (and the percentages indicated in the next three columns) to calculate the "reason" numbers shown in the respective column. We rounded the "reason" numbers to the nearest hundred.

Source: Consumer reporting agency (Agency A) data.

Using these groupings and estimated percentages, Agency A officials developed the 7-year fraud alert data presented in table 1. As indicated, the estimated number of consumers who had their credit files impacted by identity fraud increased about threefold in recent years—from an estimated 27,800 for calendar year 1995 to an estimated 89,000 for calendar year 2000. The most recent year's estimated number (89,000 consumer files in 2000) represents an increase of about 36 percent over the 1999 number (65,600).

Agency B: Number of Files with Security Alerts or Victim Statements

Agency B provides its customers two types of fraud alerts—a temporary or 90-day security alert and a 7-year victim statement. A security alert requests that a creditor ask for proof of identification before granting credit in that person's name. A victim statement provides telephone numbers supplied by the consumer and requests that creditors call the consumer before issuing credit in that person's name.

The officials explained that, if a consumer suspects a fraud-related problem, the individual is to initially call the agency's automated voice response system, which generates a 90-day security alert on the respective credit file. Agency B officials emphasized to us that most of these initial calls are not indicators that the individuals have been actual victims of fraud. Rather, the officials noted that consumers may take action to generate a 90-day security alert for a variety of reasons, such as

- reaction to a media story on identity fraud;
- a desire for added protection from identity fraud;
- suspicion of a relative, coworker, neighbor, or other person;
- an effort to get out of a legitimate debt or financial obligation; or
- a host of other reasons not related to fraud.

Also, after the 90-day security alert is generated, Agency B's policy is to provide the consumer a free copy of his or her credit file. This policy, according to Agency B officials, is to help ensure that the consumer has a better-informed basis for considering his or her situation and the need for any further action or assistance.

Upon receiving and reviewing the credit file copy, the consumer may then follow-up with the agency's call center and speak to a fraud specialist to discuss any suspicious entries on the file. In so doing, the consumer can choose to make a "victim statement," which will have the effect of extending the fraud alert from 90 days to 7 years.

Agency B officials told us that the most reliable indicator of the true incidence of identity fraud that the agency could provide is the number of 7-year victim statements placed on consumer credit files. Relevant statistics (see table 2) provided to us by Agency B indicate that the number of 7-year victim statements increased about 53 percent in recent comparative 12-month periods; that is, the number increased from 19,347 during one 12-month period (July 1999 through June 2000) to 29,593 during the more recent period (July 2000 through June 2001). Agency B officials pointed out that these numbers are relatively small compared with the numbers of initial calls that generated the 90-day security alerts. For the more recent 12-month period, for example, the number of 7-year victim statements (29,593) equates to about 2.5 percent of the initial calls that generated 90-day security alerts.

Table 2: Number of Files with Fraud Alerts Posted (Agency B), July 1999 through June 2001

Initial and follow-up calls from consumers	July 1999 through June 2000	July 2000 through June 2001	Percentage change
Initial calls that generated 90-day security alerts	1,033,180	1,198,272	+16.0
Some follow-up calls generated 7-year victim statements:			
Follow-up calls	81,041	73,096	-9.8
7-year victim statements	19,347	29,593	+53.0

Source: Consumer reporting agency (Agency B) data.

Agency C: Number of Files with Fraud Alerts

Agency C allows consumers to place temporary or 6-month fraud alerts on their credit files either by (1) using an automated voice response system and choosing the fraud option or (2) directly calling the fraud hotline and speaking with an operator at the agency's Consumer Services Center. Then, after the consumers have had the opportunity to receive and review a copy of their files, they have the option of requesting that a longer-term fraud alert be placed on their files. The duration of such an alert can range from 2 to 7 years, at the discretion of the individual consumer.

An Agency C official told us that the most reliable metric of fraud, including identity theft, is the number of files with the longer-term (2- to 7-year) fraud alerts. The official said that, in 2000, approximately 92,000 consumers called Agency C to place longer-term fraud alerts on their files. However, the official said that Agency C had no comparative statistics available for earlier years and, thus, could not make any observations about trends in the number of such fraud alerts.

The official noted that many consumers who took action to have the longer-term fraud alerts placed on their files generally had some information—such as documentation from a credit grantor, a police report, or an affidavit—indicating that they were the victims of fraud. On the other hand, the official also noted that some consumers had no direct evidence that they were victims but were uncomfortable enough with the information on their credit files to request an extended (2- to 7-year) fraud alert. The official explained that Agency C does not require consumers to submit any particular type of evidence or information in order to have these longer-term fraud alerts placed on their files.

FTC Maintains a National Database of Identity Theft Complaints

The Identity Theft and Assumption Deterrence Act of 1998 requires the FTC to "log and acknowledge the receipt of complaints by individuals who certify that they have a reasonable belief" that one or more of their means of identification have been assumed, stolen, or otherwise unlawfully acquired. In response to this requirement, in November 1999, FTC established the Identity Theft Data Clearinghouse (the FTC Clearinghouse) to gather information from any consumer who wishes to file a complaint or pose an inquiry concerning identity theft.[19] In November 1999, the first month of operation, the FTC Clearinghouse answered an average of 445 calls per week. By March 2001, the average number of calls answered had increased to over 2,000 per week. In December 2001, the weekly average was about 3,000 answered calls.

---

[19] On November 1, 1999, FTC established a toll-free telephone hotline (1-877-ID-THEFT) for consumers to report identity theft. Information from complainants is accumulated in a central database (the Identity Theft Data Clearinghouse) for use as an aid in law enforcement and prevention of identity theft.

At a congressional hearing in September 2000, an FTC official testified that Clearinghouse data demonstrate that identity theft is a "serious and growing problem."[20] Recently, during our review, FTC staff cautioned that the trend of increased calls to FTC perhaps could be attributed to a number of factors, including increased consumer awareness, and may not be due solely or primarily to an increase in the incidence of identity theft.

From its establishment in November 1999 through September 2001, the Clearinghouse received a total of 94,100 complaints from identity theft victims. As table 3 shows, five states accounted for about 44 percent of the total complaints.

Furthermore, the FTC data for November 1999 through September 2001 showed that FTC received 500 or more identity theft complaints from each of 13 cities. Of these, New York City had the highest number of complaints (3,916), followed by Chicago (1,620), Los Angeles (1,487), Houston (1,282), Miami (941), Philadelphia (695), San Francisco (621), Las Vegas (572), Phoenix (570), District of Columbia (542), San Diego (539), Dallas (537), and Atlanta (517).

Table 3: Number of Identity Theft Complaints FTC Received (Nov. 1999 through Sept. 2001) from Leading States

State	Number of complaints	Percentage
California	16,147	17.2
New York	8,219	8.7
Texas	6,775	7.2
Florida	6,309	6.7
Illinois	4,145	4.4
Subtotal	**41,595**	**44.2**
Remaining states and the District of Columbia	45,175	48.0
Other[a]	7,330	7.8
Total[b]	**94,100**	**100.0**

[a] Other refers to identity theft complaints made from U.S. territories and other countries, as well as complaints made by consumers who do not list their location.

[b] The total includes identity theft complaints forwarded from SSA/OIG to the FTC. The total does not include approximately 36,274 calls from consumers who were not identity theft victims but were seeking information about identity theft.

Source: FTC's Identity Theft Data Clearinghouse.

As table 4 shows, of the total identity theft complaints (94,100) reported to the FTC during November 1999 through September 2001, the majority of the victims (about 62 percent of the complaints) were unaware of the methods that the suspects had used to obtain the victims' personal information, and in another 18 percent of the

---

[20] FTC, prepared statement on Identity Theft, hearing before the House Committee on Banking and Financial Services (Sept. 13, 2000).

cases, this type of information was not collected. Of the remaining 19,241 complaints, or about 20 percent of the 94,100 total complaints reported to the FTC for the 23-month period, the victims provided the FTC information about the various methods used by suspects. FTC data indicated that in cases where the identity theft victim knew how the identity theft had occurred, "access through relationship with victim" (e.g., family member, neighbor, or coworker) was the most prevalent method used by suspects to obtain personal information. Specifically, this method accounted for 10,101 complaints for which the victim reported one or more methods used to obtain his or her personal information.

Table 4: Identity Theft Complaints FTC Received
(Nov. 1999 through Sept. 2001) and Categories of Methods
Suspects Used to Obtain Personal Information

Method suspects used to obtain information	Number of complaints	Percent
Method not known	58,078	61.7
Information not collected (non-FTC data[a])	16,781	17.8
Method known	19,241	20.5
Total	**94,100**	**100.0**
Method-known cases (methods of obtaining personal information were reported):	**Number of complaints**	**Percent based on subtotal[c]**
Access through relationship with victim	10,101	52.5
Wallet or purse containing identification was lost or stolen	6,615	34.4
Mail theft or fraudulent address change filed	2,577	13.4
Application, financial, or employment records compromised	1,322	6.9
Burglary or break-in	686	3.6
Internet solicitation or purchase	462	2.4
Telephone or mail solicitation or purchase	132	0.7
Other	1,706	8.9
Information about method not provided[b]	572	3.0
Subtotal	**19,241[d]**	

[a] Non-FTC data refer to identity theft complaints forwarded from SSA/OIG to the FTC. In these complaints, information about the methods suspects used was not collected.
[b] In 572 cases, consumers said that they knew but did not specify how the suspects obtained the personal information.
[c] Percentages add to more than 100 percent because some victims reported that the suspect used multiple methods of obtaining the data.
[d] Details exceed 19,241 because some victims reported that the suspect used multiple methods of obtaining data.
Source: FTC data.

Additional information about the 10,101 cases involving "access through relationship with victim" is presented in table 5. As shown, in 4,629 of the 10,101 cases where the victim knew the suspect, the victim and the suspect were family members. However, table 5 further indicates that the 10,101 cases represent less than 11 percent of the total 94,100 complaints received by the FTC during November 1999 through September 2001.

Table 5: Relationship of Suspect to Victim in Identity Theft Complaints FTC Received (Nov. 1999 through Sept. 2001)

Relationship of suspect to victim	Number of complaints	Percent based on total 94,100 complaints
Family member	4,629	0.9
Roommate/cohabitant	1,137	2.7
Neighbor	1,003	4.9
Workplace coworker/employer/employee	836	1.2
Otherwise known	2,496	1.1
Total	**10,101**	**10.7**

Source: FTC data.

SSA/OIG Fraud Hotline Statistics

SSA/OIG operates a Hotline to receive allegations of fraud, waste, and abuse. According to SSA/OIG officials, until about mid-February 2001, Hotline staff had no procedures for specifically categorizing any incoming calls as involving identity theft allegations. Rather, in recent years, the allegations most likely to involve identity theft were recorded by Hotline staff as either (1) SSN misuse or (2) program fraud, which may contain elements of SSN misuse potential. SSA/OIG officials explained these two categories of allegations as follows:

- Allegations of "SSN misuse" included, for example, incidents wherein a criminal used the SSN of another individual for the purpose of fraudulently obtaining credit, establishing utility services, or acquiring goods. Generally, this category of allegations does not directly involve SSA program benefits.

- On the other hand, allegations of fraud in SSA programs for the aged or disabled often entailed some element of SSN misuse. For example, a criminal may have used the victim's SSN or other identifying information for the purpose of obtaining Social Security benefits. When Hotline staff received this type of allegation, it was to be classified in the appropriate program fraud category, which may also have SSN misuse potential.

As shown in table 6, the number of Fraud Hotline allegations in both of these categories increased substantially in recent years. That is, the number of SSN misuse allegations increased more than fivefold, from 11,058 in fiscal year 1998 to 65,220 in fiscal year 2001, and the number of allegations of program fraud with SSN misuse potential more than doubled, from 14,542 in 1998 to 38,883 in 2001. To some extent, the increased number of allegations may be due to additional Fraud Hotline staffing, which increased from 11 to over 50 personnel during this period. However, SSA/OIG officials attributed the trend in allegations partly to a greater incidence of identity fraud.

Table 6: SSA/OIG Fraud Hotline Statistics on Allegations of SSN Misuse and Program Fraud with SSN Misuse Potential

Fiscal year	Allegations of SSN misuse	Allegations of program fraud with SSN misuse potential
1998	11,058	14,542
1999	30,116	32,260
2000	46,840	36,881
2001	65,220	38,883

Source: SSA/OIG data.

As mentioned previously, for most of the years shown in table 7, SSA/OIG had no procedures for specifically categorizing incoming calls as involving identity theft allegations. However, in 1999, SSA's Office of the Inspector General analyzed a sample of SSN misuse allegations and determined that 81.5 percent of such allegations related directly to identity theft.[21] The analysis covered a statistical sample of 400 allegations from a universe of 16,375 SSN misuse allegations received by the SSA/OIG Fraud Hotline from October 1997 through March 1999. The analysis did not cover the other category presented in table 6, that is, allegations of program fraud with SSN misuse potential.

Recently, in about mid-February 2001, SSA/OIG implemented procedures to routinely and specifically determine which Fraud Hotline allegations of SSN misuse involve identity theft.[22] For example, as table 7 shows, for 7 months (Mar. through Sept.) in 2001, the Fraud Hotline received 25,991 identity theft allegations, which are arrayed among 16 categories. As shown, the most prevalent identity theft category involved credit cards, which accounted for 9,488 allegations or almost 37 percent of the total identity theft allegations. The next highest identity theft category—about

---

[21] SSA, Office of the Inspector General, *Management Advisory Report – Analysis of Social Security Number Misuse Allegations Made to the Social Security Administration's Fraud Hotline* (A-15-99-92019, Aug. 1999).

[22] The procedures do not cover allegations of program fraud with SSN misuse potential.

4,600 employment-related allegations—usually involved illegal aliens, according to SSA/OIG officials.

Table 7: SSA/OIG Fraud Hotline Statistics on Allegations of SSN Misuse That Directly Involve Identity Theft (by Category), March through September 2001

Identity theft category	Number of allegations	Percentage
Credit card	9,488	36.5
Employment	4,637	17.8
Lost/stolen SSN information (wallet/purse)[a]	3,421	13.2
Bank fraud	2,765	10.6
Utility	2,761	10.6
Tax return	1,032	4.0
Medical care	548	2.1
Driver's license	496	1.9
Housing	224	0.9
Child support	171	0.7
Internet	157	0.6
Government loan	93	0.4
Bankruptcy	83	0.3
INS document	79	0.3
Birth certificate	24	0.1
Passport	12	0.0
Total	**25,991**	**100.0**

Note: According to the SSA/OIG, the identity theft categories reflect the most applicable primary allegation code assigned by the individual SSA program specialist who originally received the allegation. Also, the SSA/OIG noted that the accuracy of the categorizations cannot be confirmed until an allegation is investigated; only about 10 percent of all allegations are opened as investigative cases. Furthermore, the SSA/OIG noted that its identity theft codes do not include certain categories, such as counterfeit SSN cards, trafficking counterfeit SSN cards, trafficking legitimate SSN cards, and false statement to obtain SSN.

[a] The SSA/OIG began using this primary allegation code in June 2001. The SSA/OIG indicated that the code is used for reports of a lost or stolen SSN card where the caller is concerned that his or her SSN may be used fraudulently, but no information is provided to indicate that the SSN has in fact been misused and no loss has been suffered.

Source: SSA/OIG data.

During this 7-month period, the number of identity theft allegations per month increased about 40 percent, from 3,028 in March 2001 to 4,258 in September 2001.

Department of Justice Law Enforcement Components

Regarding Department of Justice law enforcement actions (e.g., number of investigations, arrests, and prosecutions), we obtained identity theft-related statistics from the Executive Office for U.S. Attorneys (EOUSA) and the Federal Bureau of Investigation (FBI).

EOUSA Data

For fiscal years 1996 through 2000, EOUSA provided us with statistics on the number of cases filed under federal statutes related to identity fraud. As indicated in table 8:

- The number of cases filed under 18 U.S.C. § 1028 reflect year-to-year increases and more than doubled from 314 cases in 1996 to 775 cases in 2000.

- The number of cases filed under 18 U.S.C. § 1029 reflect a general decrease, and the most recent figure—703 cases in 2000—is considerably lower than the 924 cases filed in 1996.

- The number of cases filed under 42 U.S.C. § 408 reflect a general increase. The number of cases filed increased substantially in 1998, when compared with the previous 2 years. And, the number of cases filed in 2000 was more than double the number filed in 1996.

Table 8: U.S. Attorney Cases Filed Under Statutes Related to Identity Fraud

Fiscal year	18 U.S.C. § 1028 (Identification documents)	18 U.S.C. § 1029 (Access devices)	42 U.S.C. § 408 (SSN misuse)
1996	314	924	310
1997	404	864	308
1998	550	752	576
1999	568	675	558
2000	775	703	694

Source: EOUSA data.

Also, in reference to table 8, EOUSA staff made the following clarifying comments:

- A given case may be counted under more than one of the three U.S. Code sections because a defendant could have been charged with multiple offenses. However, in table 8's statistics for case filings, there is no double counting of multiple charges of the same Code section, nor of filings under the subsections of that section. For instance, if a defendant was charged with two counts of violations under 18 U.S.C. § 1028(a)(7) in one case, the relevant statistics would still appear as only one case under the 18 U.S.C. § 1028 column in table 8.

- EOUSA has only limited statistical information available at the subsection level or the sub-subsection level for offenses charged under title 18 of the U.S. Code. Except for certain firearms statutes, the case management system requests that cases be recorded under the U.S. Code section only, not under the subsection or the sub-subsection, although this additional information sometimes is provided. Thus, these "subsection-level or sub-subsection-level statistics" have great potential for underreporting. Also, cases involving identity theft or identity fraud are charged under a variety of different statutes, and many criminals who commit identity theft are charged under statutes relating to these defendants' other crimes. With these significant limitations or caveats in mind, EOUSA data indicated that, of the 568 cases filed under 18 U.S.C. § 1028 in fiscal year 1999, the number of cases with at least one charge of a violation of subsection (a)(7) recorded in the EOUSA data base was 24 cases. And, for fiscal year 2000, of the 775 cases filed under 18 U.S.C. § 1028, the number of cases with at least one charge of a violation of subsection (a)(7) recorded in the EOUSA data base was 68 cases.

FBI Data

At the time of our review, FBI officials told us that the agency did not have the capability to determine the number of statistical accomplishments (e.g., arrests and convictions) that have resulted from 18 U.S.C. § 1028(a)(7). The officials noted, however, that the agency was in the process of developing a system to track the number of cases that included identity theft as a component.

Moreover, regarding case statistics that were presently available, the FBI officials offered the following contextual considerations:

- Even if accomplishments from investigative cases could be isolated or tracked to the 1998 act, these cases would not necessarily be an accurate reflection on this law. For instance, an open issue would be to determine if these cases would have been prosecuted using other equally beneficial statutes or not at all.

- Cases involving identity theft or identity fraud typically are classified by the crimes committed using the stolen fraudulent identity—classified, for example, as bank fraud, wire fraud, or mail fraud. In other words, an individual may not always be charged with identity theft but instead be charged with the substantive violations carried out using the stolen identity.

- As other possibilities, a prosecutor may allow an individual who was charged with identity theft to plead guilty to other criminal conduct charges.

With these considerations in mind, the FBI provided us with statistics showing the agency's accomplishments under identity theft-related statutes. Table 9 summarizes the statistics for fiscal years 1996-2001. As indicated, much of the FBI's enforcement activities involved bank fraud cases, which is an area of longstanding responsibility for the FBI.

Table 9: FBI Accomplishments Under Identity Theft-Related Statutes, Fiscal Years 1996 through 2001

Statute	1996	1997	1998	1999	2000	2001[a]
18 U.S.C. § 1028 (Identification documents)						
Indictments and informations[b]	33	33	22	55	99	49
Arrests	24	17	20	28	40	43
Convictions	33	27	17	21	50	29
18 U.S.C. § 1029 (Access devices)						
Indictments and informations[b]	90	95	114	96	125	39
Arrests	38	60	78	69	90	35
Convictions	60	80	77	105	74	35
18 U.S.C. § 1014 (Loan and credit applications)						
Indictments and informations[b]	311	290	235	189	206	94
Arrests	58	62	72	38	85	38
Convictions	304	242	170	146	121	50
18 U.S.C. § 1344 (bank fraud)						
Indictments and informations[b]	1,225	1,159	1,305	1,492	1,481	626
Arrests	311	468	579	691	645	311
Convictions	1,121	896	983	1,047	1,112	449
42 U.S.C. § 408 (SSN misuse)						
Indictments and informations[b]	85	75	97	119	98	40
Arrests	25	15	40	48	62	22
Convictions	61	50	62	64	68	23
15 U.S.C. § 1644 (fraudulent use of credit cards)						
Indictments and informations[b]	11	1	1	1	1	1
Arrests	2	0	1	0	0	2
Convictions	5	2	2	0	0	1

[a] Fiscal year 2001 numbers are as of April 10, 2001.
[b] Generally, an indictment is an accusation presented in writing by a grand jury, charging a person for some criminal offense, whereas an information is presented by a competent public officer on his or her oath of office.
Source: FBI data.

Department of the Treasury Law Enforcement Components

Regarding Department of the Treasury law enforcement actions, we obtained identity theft-related statistics from the Internal Revenue Service (IRS), the Secret Service, and the Financial Crimes Enforcement Network (FinCEN).

IRS: Many Questionable Refund Schemes Involve Identity Theft

According to the IRS, many questionable refund schemes involve an element of identity theft or identity fraud. However, IRS emphasized that not all questionable refund schemes involve this element. For instance, IRS noted that many false returns are filed by the true taxpayer using false income documents (e.g., W-2s, W-2Gs, and Forms 4852 and 1099) with inflated income and/or withholding.

IRS-Criminal Investigation does not routinely keep statistics as to how many questionable refund schemes and questionable returns involve some element of identity theft or identity fraud. Thus, IRS told us that it is difficult to determine the specific number of schemes, refunds, claims, and dollar losses that are solely attributable to identity theft or fraud.

With these caveats in mind and in response to our request, IRS-Criminal Investigation's Office of Refund Crimes developed statistics to reflect its "best effort to show the prevalence of identity fraud." That is, for calendar years 1996 through 2000, IRS provided us with statistics covering all questionable refund schemes that IRS classified as involving a "high frequency" of identity theft or identity fraud—schemes very likely to have elements of this type of crime (see table 10). In 2000, for example, IRS detected a total of 3,085 such schemes, consisting of 35,185 questionable tax returns that claimed a total of $783 million in refunds. According to IRS officials, the agency's detection efforts in that year prevented payment of $757 million.

Table 10: Questionable Refund Schemes Detected by IRS

Dollars in millions

Calendar year	Questionable refund schemes	Questionable returns detected	Refunds claimed	Refunds stopped
1996	2,458	24,919	$82	$69
1997	2,857	30,936	108	95
1998	2,810	31,155	98	77
1999	2,406	31,532	689	667
2000	3,085	35,185	783	757
Total	13,616	153,727	$1,760	$1,665

Source: IRS, Criminal Investigation.

Secret Service Data

According to the Secret Service, the vast majority of financial crimes involve the use of some sort of false identification, the use of another individual's personal or financial identifiers, or the assumption of a false or fictitious identity. In explanation, Secret Service officials noted the following:

- Broadly speaking, from the perspective of law enforcement, identity theft can involve either "account takeover" or "identity takeover." That is, such theft involves the use of personal information to (1) make unauthorized use of existing credit or other financial accounts or (2) establish new accounts, apply for loans, etc. Generally, the personal information often sought by criminals is information required to obtain goods and services on credit. Primary types of this information include names, dates of birth, and SSNs. With the proliferation of computers and increased use of the Internet, many identity thieves have used information obtained from company databases and Web sites.

- Identity theft is not typically a "stand alone" crime. Rather, identity theft is almost always a component of one or more crimes, such as bank fraud, credit card or access device fraud, or the use of counterfeit financial instruments. In many instances, an identity theft case encompasses several different types of fraud.

In further response to our inquiry, Secret Service officials said that they believe that identity theft continues to occur at a seemingly increasing pace. The officials cautioned, however, that the incidence of identity theft is difficult to measure on the basis of available statistics (such as number of investigations or arrests) for a variety of reasons. Among others, the reasons cited were lack of reporting by victims, classification of identity theft in other crime categories (e.g., theft or forgery) or perhaps as a civil matter, and different levels of law enforcement (federal, state, and local) having concurrent jurisdiction with respect to many aspects of identity theft. Given these limitations, the officials suggested that any assessment of overall trends regarding identity theft perhaps should be based on statistics from FTC—the agency designated to be the primary point of contact for victims.

Nonetheless, we obtained available statistics from the Secret Service regarding its identity-theft related cases for fiscal years 1998-2000 (see table 11). In interpreting these data, Secret Service officials noted that, in recent years, the agency has moved away from investigating "street crime" level offenders in the identity theft spectrum to targeting individuals and groups engaged in the systematic, large-scale pursuit of profits through the commission of various types of identity theft. That is, the agency is now focusing on high-dollar, community-impact cases that merit federal interest. Case statistics for fiscal years 1998-2000 reflect this shift in focus, according to Secret Service officials, who noted the following:

- The number of arrests decreased 28 percent from 1998 to 2000, and the number of cases closed dropped 37 percent.

- On the other hand, the average actual losses to victims in closed cases rose 71 percent from 1998 to 2000. The average fraud losses prevented rose 48 percent from 1998 to 1999 and rose an additional 101 percent from 1999 to 2000.

Table 11: Secret Service Data on Identity Theft-Related Arrests, Cases Closed, and Dollar Losses in Fiscal Years 1998 through 2000

Data category	1998	1999	2000
Arrests	4,421	3,814	3,163
Cases closed[a]	8,489	7,071	5,379
Average actual losses to victims in cases closed[b]	$26,922	$38,078	$46,119
Average fraud losses prevented in cases closed[c]	$73,382	$108,476	$217,696

Note: In compiling these data, the Secret Service defined identity theft as any case related to the investigation of false, fraudulent, or counterfeit identification; stolen, counterfeit, or altered checks or Treasury securities; stolen, altered, or counterfeit credit cards; or financial institution fraud.

[a] Cases can be closed for a variety of reasons, such as completion of judicial action, declination to prosecute by the Office of the United States Attorney, or a determination that insufficient evidence exists to identify or charge a suspect.

[b] As defined by the Secret Service, "actual losses" are the amounts of money, goods, or services that were obtained by the criminal or group of criminals through the commission of the crime.

[c] As defined by the Secret Service, "fraud losses prevented" is the difference between potential losses and actual losses. The Service defined "potential losses" as the amounts of money, goods, or services that the criminal or group of criminals was trying to obtain through the commission of the crime.

Source: Secret Service data.

FinCEN Data

In April 1996, financial institutions were required to begin filing suspicious activity reports (SAR) to assist law enforcement in detecting and prosecuting violations of money laundering and other financial crimes.[23] Recently, to "provide insights into the patterns of criminal financial activity associated with identity theft," FinCEN analyzed SARs filed during the period April 1996 through November 2000— a total of 490,595 filings. Of this total, FinCEN's analysis indicated that 1,030 SARs reported identity y theft. Analysis of these 1,030 SARs, according to FinCEN's June 2001 report, confirms "industry perceptions of increases in both the incidence of

---

[23] The SAR system replaced a "criminal referral reporting" system that had been used since 1984.

identity theft-based fraud and SAR reporting about the phenomenon."[24] Specifically, FinCEN noted the following:

- During January through December 1997, the first full year of required SAR reporting, 44 instances of identity theft—fewer than 4 per month—were reported.
- Recently, during January through November 2000, there were 617 SARs filed that reported identity theft, an average of 56 SARs per month.

Also, in its report, FinCEN noted—but did not elaborate or provide related statistics—that advanced technology (particularly the Internet) is proving to be a "powerful facilitator" of identity theft.

Postal Inspection Service

The Postal Inspection Service is a leading federal law enforcement agency in the investigation of identity takeovers, a crime that frequently begins with the theft of mail or use of the mail to defraud individuals or financial institutions. In its fiscal year 2000 annual report, the Postal Inspection Service noted that identity theft is a growing trend:

"Inspection Service identity theft investigations increased by 67 percent since last year. Identity theft occurs when mail is stolen for the personal information it contains, which criminals use to fraudulently order credit cards, checks or other financial instruments. Mail theft may go unreported—the thief looks for mail containing items such as a credit card payment, copies personal identifiers and credit card and bank account information, and reseals the envelope and returns it to the mailstream, often undetected. Checks and credit cards may then be ordered in the victim's name. Private mailboxes at commercial receiving agencies ... are often rented so the crook can receive the fraudulently obtained cards and checks anonymously."[25]

Also, in its 2000 annual report, the Postal Inspection Service mentioned various initiatives to address identity theft:

"Credit card theft and identity theft are becoming increasingly intertwined as crimes involving the U.S. Mail. The U.S. Postal Inspection Service's Credit Card Mail Security Initiative has brought various federal law enforcement agencies and credit card industry representatives together since 1992 to discuss loss and theft issues and

---

[24] FinCEN, *The SAR Activity Review—Trends, Tips & Issues*, Issue 2 (June 2001), p. 14.
[25] *2000 Annual Report of Investigations of the United States Postal Inspection Service* (Nov. 2000), p. 9.

develop solutions. Many of the identity theft issues related to credit card losses are currently being addressed by members of the initiative. ...

"On November 6, 1999, President Clinton announced the Know Fraud initiative, a partnership of several leading private and government agencies, including the U.S. Postal Inspection Service, to educate consumers about how to protect themselves from telemarketing and mail fraud. ... Although work continues on the first Know Fraud initiative, plans are underway for a second one to launch in early 2001. Focusing on identity theft, the goal of the new effort is to deliver to every home in America prevention information that will raise awareness of this growing trend and provide consumers with protective tactics."[26]

According to the Postal Inspection Service, the "Know Fraud" initiative is "the largest consumer protection effort ever undertaken, with postcards sent to 123 million addresses across America, arming consumers with common sense tips and guidelines ..."

Postal Inspection Service arrest statistics indicate that the agency has increased its focus on identity theft-related crime in recent years (see table 12). For instance, whereas the annual number of arrests was relatively constant during fiscal years 1996 through 1999, the year 2000 total (1,722 arrests) represents an increase of about 36 percent over the previous year. Furthermore, the total for partial-year 2001 (9 months) is higher than the year 2000 total.

Table 12: Postal Inspection Service Identity Theft-Related Arrests, Fiscal Years 1996 through 2001

Fiscal year	Number of arrests
1996	1,287
1997	1,226
1998	1,122
1999	1,267
2000	1,722
2001 (through June 30, 2001)	1,752

Source: Postal Inspection Service data.

---

[26] *2000 Annual Report of Investigations of the United States Postal Inspection Service* (Nov. 2000), pp. 9, 40-41.

APPENDIX II: COST OF IDENTITY THEFT TO THE FINANCIAL SERVICES INDUSTRY

According to industry data, the dollar value of goods and services purchased by consumers in the United States was $6.8 trillion in the year 2000. General purpose credit cards—American Express, Diners Club, Discover, MasterCard, and Visa—were used to pay for 20.4 percent of these consumption expenditures.[27] MasterCard and Visa comprised about 76 percent of the U.S. card market share, based on first quarter 2001 data. Also, as members of the MasterCard and Visa associations, much of the banking industry engaged in issuing credit cards, as well as offering checking accounts.

This appendix discusses identity theft and the financial services industry in reference to three categories or aspects of cost—direct fraud losses, staffing and operating cost of fraud departments, and consumer confidence in online commerce (i.e., e-commerce through the Internet).

Direct Fraud Losses

Regarding identity theft-related direct fraud losses incurred by the financial services industry, we obtained information from (1) the American Bankers Association (ABA); (2) the two leading payment card associations, MasterCard and Visa; and (3) six credit card-issuing banks.[28]

ABA Check Fraud Survey

In its 2000 bank industry survey on check fraud, the ABA reported that total check fraud-related losses in 1999—considering both actual losses ($679 million) and loss avoidance ($1.5 billion)—against commercial bank accounts reached $2.2 billion, which was twice the amount in 1997.[29] Regarding actual losses, the report noted that the 1999 figure ($679 million) was up almost 33 percent from the 1997 estimate ($512 million).

---

[27] Checks were used to pay for 51.3 percent of total consumption expenditures, cash was used for 16.7 percent, other proprietary cards for 4.1 percent, and "other" (such as money orders) for 7.6 percent. (Details add to 100.1 percent due to rounding.)

[28] As discussed in appendix I, these banks are among the top 14 credit-card issuing banks in terms of managed receivables. Of the top-issuing group of 14 banks, we were able to arrange in-person or telephone interviews with officials of 6 banks.

[29] ABA, *Deposit Account Fraud Survey Report 2000*, p. 9. ABA conducted its survey between February and June 2000 and received responses (completed survey forms) from 542 commercial banks. According to the ABA, the reported loss figures represent extrapolations to the industry level. ABA defined "loss avoidance" as the amount of losses avoided as a result of the banks' prevention systems and procedures.

In 1999, according to ABA data shown in table 13, the percentages of total check fraud-related losses attributable to identity theft ranged from 56 percent at community banks to 5 percent at superregional/money center banks. To restate, at the high end of this range, community banks reported that 56 percent of their check fraud-related losses could be attributed to identity theft; and at the low end of the range, superregional/money center banks reported that 5 percent of their check fraud-related losses could be attributed to identity theft. As previously mentioned, the ABA reported that check fraud-related losses totaled $2.2 billion in 1999. However, the ABA's report did not specifically disaggregate this total among the bank-size categories shown in table 13.

Table 13: Percentages of Banks' Total Check Fraud-Related Losses Attributable to Identity Theft, 1999

Banks (by size based on assets)	Identity theft losses as a percentage of total check fraud-related losses
Community banks (assets under $500 million)	56
Mid-size banks (assets of $500 million to under $5 billion)	18
Regional banks (assets of $5 billion to under $50 billion)	6
Superregional/money center banks (assets of $50 billion or more)	5
All sizes combined	29

Note: ABA defined identity theft as losses due to account takeovers (or true name fraud). The overall response rate for ABA's survey was 11 percent. The response rates by bank size were as follows: community banks (10 percent), mid-size banks (16 percent), regional banks (27 percent), and superregional/money center banks (65 percent). Surveys with a low level of responses—particularly surveys with response rates lower than 50 percent—could be affected by nonresponse bias. Thus, the results from ABA's survey should be interpreted with caution.

Source: ABA, *Deposit Account Fraud Survey Report 2000*, p. 19.

In the same report, banks surveyed by the ABA between February and June 2000 identified the leading threats against deposit accounts anticipated in the next 12 months. The leading threat category cited by the surveyed banks involved counterfeit checks, and this category was closely followed by concerns regarding debit cards, identity theft (true name fraud), and the Internet. The percentages of surveyed banks that ranked identity theft among the top three threats against deposit accounts, as shown in table 14, ranged from a low of 48.4 percent of community banks to a high of 75.8 percent of regional banks.

Table 14: Percentage of Banks that Regard Identity Theft (True Name Fraud) as One of the Top Three Threats Against Deposit Accounts

Banks (by size based on assets)	Percentage of surveyed banks
Community banks (assets under $500 million)	48.4
Mid-size banks (assets of $500 million to under $5 billion)	60.2
Regional banks (assets of $5 billion to under $50 billion)	75.8
Superregional/money center banks (assets of $50 billion or more)	63.6

Note: ABA defined identity theft as losses due to account takeovers (or true name fraud). The overall response rate for ABA's survey was 11 percent. The response rates by bank size were as follows: community banks (10 percent), mid-size banks (16 percent), regional banks (27 percent), and superregional/money center banks (65 percent). Surveys with a low level of responses—particularly surveys with response rates lower than 50 percent—could be affected by nonresponse bias. Thus, the results from ABA's survey should be interpreted with caution.

Source: ABA Data.

Two Major Payment Card Associations: Fraud Losses Involving Identity Theft

MasterCard and Visa are separate associations owned by numerous financial institutions that issue payment cards (credit cards and debit cards) bearing the MasterCard name and the Visa name, respectively. As such, MasterCard and Visa rarely receive complaints of fraud directly from consumers. Rather, the fraud-related statistics that MasterCard and Visa report represent an aggregation of data reported by each association's members. Association members report fraud-related statistics in various categories, such as account takeovers, fraudulent applications, lost cards, stolen cards, never-received cards, counterfeit cards, and mail order/telephone order fraud.

Regarding these various categories, MasterCard and Visa use very similar (although not identical) definitions regarding which of these categories constitute identity theft, as opposed to other types of fraud. According to a MasterCard official, the identity theft-related categories are account takeovers and some portion of fraudulent applications. A Visa official said that two categories—account takeovers and fraudulent applications—are considered by Visa to be identity theft because the other forms of fraud do not necessarily require the "stealing" of another person's identifying information.[30]

In response to our inquiry, MasterCard and Visa officials provided us with information on their respective association's fraud-related dollar losses for calendar years 1996 through 2000. However, the officials considered this information to be

---

[30] In contrast to these relatively narrow definitions, the Secret Service, as a lead federal enforcement agency for identity theft, defines this crime more broadly to encompass virtually all categories of payment card fraud.

proprietary and requested that we aggregate the data in our reporting rather than present association-specific data. We agreed. The associations' aggregated data are presented in table 15. As indicated, for domestic (U.S.) operations, the associations' identity theft-related fraud losses—defined as involving account takeovers and fraudulent applications—rose from $79.9 million in 1996 to $114.3 million in 2000, an increase of about 43 percent. Much of this increase is reflected in the account-takeover losses, which increased more than twofold, from $33.0 million in 1996 to $68.2 million in 2000. An official of one association said that this increase probably could be attributed to "inconsistencies in reporting among member banks." The official added that consumers are not really at risk because a zero liability policy protects them from financial loss.

Furthermore, table 15 shows that the associations' identity theft-related losses as a percentage of total fraud losses were relatively constant at about 9 to 10 percent during 1996 through 2000. In further perspective, for most of these years, table 15 shows that the associations' total fraud losses represented less than 1/10th of 1 percent of U.S. member banks' sales volume. Generally, the fraud losses are borne by the financial institution that issued the payment card. In some instances, although reportedly rare, retail merchants may bear such losses if the merchants do not follow proper procedures for verifying use of the card.

Table 15: MasterCard and Visa Fraud Losses, Calendar Years 1996 through 2000

Dollars in millions					
Fraud losses by category	**1996**	**1997**	**1998**	**1999**	**2000**
Identity theft-related losses:					
Account takeovers[a]	$33.1	$32.4	$34.4	$39.8	$68.2
Fraudulent applications[b]	46.8	36.9	37.2	43.4	46.1
Subtotal	**$79.9**	**$69.3**	**$71.6**	**$83.3**	**$114.3**
Additional fraud losses[c]	620.3	590.4	663.9	700.8	898.9
Total fraud losses	**$700.2**	**659.7**	**735.5**	**784.1**	**$1,013.2**
Identity theft-related losses as a percentage of total fraud losses	11.4%	10.5	9.7	10.6	11.3
Total fraud losses as a percentage of associations' U.S. members' sales volume	0.104%	0.084%	0.081%	0.074%	0.082%

[a] A Visa official said that the account takeover category may include some miscellaneous fraud losses reported by Visa member banks; thus, the dollar losses attributed to account takeovers may be somewhat overstated.
[b] According to a MasterCard official, the fraudulent applications category can have components that do not involve identity theft.
[c] Additional fraud losses include categories such as lost and stolen cards, never-received cards, counterfeit cards, and mail order/telephone order fraud.
Source: MasterCard and Visa data for domestic (U.S.) operations.

To reiterate, regarding direct fraud losses involving payment cards, we contacted MasterCard and Visa only. We did not obtain information about losses involving other general-purpose cards (American Express, Diners Club, and Discover), which account for about 25 percent of the market. Also, we did not obtain information about losses involving merchantspecific cards issued by retail stores. Furthermore, we did not obtain information from various entities, such as insurance companies and securities firms, which may incur identity theft-related costs.

An official of one of the associations told us that identity theft is not perceived to be one of the biggest fraud-related problems faced by member banks. The official said that many banks have experience in dealing with identity fraud, including using new technology to detect where such fraud may be taking place. Additionally, to help reduce the incidence of fraud, the official noted that the association provides guidance or recommendations for member banks and merchants to follow, as well as a number of specific computer models and authorization and verification systems that help reduce fraud and identity theft.

Selected Credit Card-Issuing Banks

Officials of six credit card-issuing banks that we contacted said their financial institutions track fraud in several categories. But, we found some inconsistency among these institutions on the definition of credit card fraud associated with identity theft. For example, some financial institutions did not consider "friendly fraud" or "family fraud"[31] in their fraud losses to be related to identity theft. However, two categories of identity theft-related fraud used by all six banks were (1) fraudulent applications and (2) account takeovers. Five of the six banks had data on identity theft losses involving fraudulent applications and account takeovers. These losses ranged from 18 percent to 42 percent of the respective bank's overall fraud losses.[32] However, bank officials acknowledged that identity theft could also be associated with lost or stolen payment cards or other categories of losses—and, thus, the reporting of losses for only two categories (fraudulent applications and account takeovers) may understate total identity theft-related losses.

Officials from one of the six banks said that the amount of losses is not large, and the bank considered these losses to be within an acceptable level of risk. Also, the officials noted that the bank experienced more fraud from unauthorized use—that is, use of lost or stolen cards and forged checks—than from account takeovers and fraudulent applications.

---

[31] Friendly or family fraud could occur when there is an unauthorized use of a credit card or personal information by an acquaintance, friend, or family member. Friends or family members sometimes apply for credit in the victim's name or take over existing accounts in cases of death or disability without notifying the financial institution. In these cases, financial institutions are usually able to recover their losses or shift the responsibility for existing accounts.

[32] The sixth bank did not provide us with data reflecting identity theft losses as a percentage of overall fraud losses.

Officials from a second bank said that their bank's largest source of credit card fraud was from lost or stolen credit cards. The officials added that the next most common form of fraud involved counterfeit credit cards—a type of fraudulent activity that occurred worldwide and often was perpetrated by organized crime rings. The third most common form of fraud—and more difficult to detect—was account takeover. The root cause of identity theft associated with account takeover, according to these bank officials, involved the misuse of SSNs acquired from another source. Also, this bank reported having experienced an increase in the number of cases of friendly fraud—that is, incidents whereby a victim's family member or acquaintances obtained or tried to obtain credit in the victim's name. For example, in a divorce situation, a spouse may have opened an account in his or her partner's name without consent.

Officials from a third bank said that the growth of fraud losses was correlated to business growth. However, the officials noted that the bank's losses associated with identity theft had remained relatively constant during the last few years.

Officials at a fourth bank said that the bank does not normally track identity theft. Rather, the bank tracked the number of fraudulent applications denied due to the suspicion of fraud. Regarding this category, the bank officials did not consider the number of incidents to be significant in relationship to the bank's overall customer base; however, the officials noted that cases often occurred in "waves." Moreover, the officials said that they were concerned with larger losses, which resulted from fraudulent activities perpetrated by organized crime rings.

At a fifth bank, officials said that roughly 90 percent of the bank's identity theft cases involved fraudulent applications, and the remainder represented account takeovers. The officials explained that, when the bank focuses on combating one form of fraudulent activity, other or replacement manifestations often begin to appear. For instance, the officials noted that fraud had increased from credit cards not received in the mail. In addition, the officials said they believed that fraudulent activity associated with organized crime rings was on the rise.

At the sixth bank, officials provided no additional information about the institution's fraud losses.

STAFFING AND COST OF FRAUD DEPARTMENTS

The following sections discuss the staffing and cost of the fraud departments of banks and CRAs. The sections present information based on (1) ABA's 2000 bank industry survey on check fraud, (2) responses from officials of various banks we contacted, and (3) our interviews with officials of the three national CRAs.

ABA Data: Fraud-Related Operating Expenses of Banks

In its 2000 bank industry survey on check fraud, the ABA reported that the amount of resources that banks devoted to check fraud prevention, detection, investigation, and prosecution varied as a direct function of bank size. For instance, as table 16 shows for check fraud-related operating expenses (not including actual losses) in 1999,

- over two-thirds (69.5 percent) of the 446 community banks that responded to ABA's survey each incurred less than $10,000 for such expenses;
- about one-third (32.0 percent) of the 103 responding mid-size banks each incurred such expenses ranging from $50,000 to $249,999;
- about one-fourth (24.2 percent) of the 33 responding regional banks each incurred such expenses ranging from $500,000 to $999,999. Another one-fourth of the regional banks each incurred such expenses ranging from $1 million to $4.9 million; and
- about one-fourth (27.3 percent) of the 11 responding superregional/money center banks each incurred more than $10 million for such expenses.

Table 16: Amount of Expenses Per Bank Devoted to Prevention, Detection, Investigation, and Prosecution of Check Fraud, 1999

Expenses per bank	Community banks (assets under $500 million)	Mid-size banks (assets of $500 million to under $5 billion)	Regional banks (assets of $5 billion to under $50 billion)	Superregional / money center banks (assets of $50 billion or more)
Less than $10,000	69.5%	24.3%	—	—
$10,000 to $49,999	9.6	21.4	—	—
$50,000 to $249,999	1.3	32.0	21.2%	—
$250,000 to $499,999	—	4.9	18.2	—
$500,000 to $999,999	—	—	24.2	18.2%
$1 million to $4.9 million	—	1.0	24.2	27.3
$5 million to $9.9 million	—	—	—	9.1
$10 million or more	—	—	—	27.3
Do not know	19.5	16.5	12.1	18.2
Totals[a]	**99.9%**	**100.1%**	**99.9%**	**100.1%**
Number of banks responding	446	103	33	11

[a] Percentages do not add to 100.0 percent due to rounding.
Source: ABA, *Deposit Account Fraud Survey Report 2000*, p. 60.

Fraud Departments of Selected Banks

The six banks discussed earlier also responded to our questions about fraud department staffing. Bank officials expressed concern about the growing sophistication of identity thieves, and the officials indicated that their respective banks had taken a number of proprietary steps for preventing, detecting, and responding to fraud. The officials told us that fraud department staffing had increased over the last few years, both in relationship to the growth in business portfolios and to address increasing fraud losses. However, the officials said that they could not specifically quantify the fraud department costs associated with identity theft. Rather, the information provided to us can be summarized as follows:

- At four of the six banks, officials reported that fraud department staffing had expanded, with designated or specialized staff devoted to dealing with fraud prevention. The officials noted that their respective bank's fraud prevention procedures were dynamic and proprietary.

- At a fifth bank, officials told us that about 30 percent of the fraud unit's employees were associated with addressing identity theft. The officials added that the unit's staffing had increased over the last 5 years, in line with the bank's portfolio growth. However, the officials also said they had witnessed an increase in fraudulent applications—concurrent with an increase in Web site usage—and had taken additional preventative steps to address such applications.

- At the sixth bank, officials told us that fraud department staffing had remained relatively stable over the last 5 years.

Moreover, in addition to fraud department staffing, various bank officials indicated that there were other indirect costs associated with addressing identity theft. Examples of such costs included the following:

- To assist in correcting credit bureau files, banks devote resources to communicating with customers and CRAs.

- Banks use resources in cooperating with law enforcement agents who investigate identity theft crimes. And, expenses are incurred in attempts to locate perpetrators, bill them, and collect owed amounts.

- Banks may incur lost opportunity costs in not being able to extend credit to legitimate customers.

Fraud-Assistance Staffing at the Three National CRAs

Officials from each of the three national CRAs told us that the number of fraud-assistance staff—that is, staff to answer telephone calls and correspondence from individuals who believed that they may have been the victims of fraud—had increased in recent years. In obtaining staffing information from the three national CRAs, we agreed to report the information in a manner not specifically identifiable to the respective agency. Thus, in the following sections, we refer to these sources as "Agency A," "Agency B," and "Agency C." Of the three, Agency A and Agency C had a call center devoted specifically to fraud assistance. Agency B's call center handled both fraud-related and nonfraud-related matters, such as various types of consumer inquiries and disputes.

Agency A: Fraud-Assistance Staffing Has Doubled

An Agency A official said that the number of staff in the agency's fraud assistance department doubled in recent years, increasing from 50 in 1997 to 103 in 2001. In discussing the reasons for this increase, the official explained that greater public awareness of identity theft has resulted in a much larger volume of calls from consumers to the CRA. Now, the official opined, virtually any person who has a wallet or purse stolen will call a CRA as a protective measure against becoming a fraud victim.

Moreover, the official said that Agency A's operating policy is to have a sufficient number of fraud-assistance staff available so that consumers will be able to speak with someone when they first telephone. In contrast, the official noted that the other two CRAs have an automated response system for handling the initial telephone inquiries from consumers. Thus, the official said that Agency A has a greater number of fraud-assistance staff than the other two CRAs.

According to this official, Agency A's staffing costs for the fraud assistance department were about $3.3 million in 2000. Adding administrative costs to the staffing costs, the official said that the department's total operating costs for the year exceeded $4 million.

Agency B: Fraud-Assistance Staffing Has Increased

Agency B officials provided us with information that was more general or less specific than that provided by Agency A. That is, the officials said that:

- Agency B's fraud-assistance staffing has increased in recent years and remained relatively steady at 30 to 40 fraud specialists in 2000 and 2001.

- The annual cost of maintaining a staff of fraud-assistance specialists is in the range of "several million dollars."

Also, in discussing Agency B's automated response system for handling initial inquiries, the officials said that the system has the advantage of being available to consumers 24 hours a day, 7 days a week. The officials explained Agency B's system as follows:

- When a consumer telephones the CRA, the automated system gives a menu of various options, one of which is a fraud-assistance option. If a consumer selects this option, Agency B automatically places a 90-day security alert on the consumer's file.

- In addition to being provided a credit file report, the consumer is given a toll-free telephone number that the consumer can call to discuss—with Agency B fraud-assistance staff—the report and any related fraud concerns. In calling and discussing his or her situation, the consumer may choose to make a "victim statement," which will have the effect of extending the fraud alert to a period of 7 years. Upon adding the victim statement, an updated credit report will be sent to the consumer, and two more reports will be provided at 45-day intervals.

According to these officials, another advantage of Agency B's automated response system for handling a consumer's initial inquiry is that the credit file reports give the consumer a basis for subsequently having a more informed discussion with the agency's fraud-assistance staff. Finally, the officials noted that the free reports—which total over 1 million annually—represent a significant but easily overlooked cost of identity fraud to CRAs.

Agency C: Fraud-Assistance Staffing Has Increased

An Agency C official provided us with information on the approximate costs and hotline staffing levels for the fraud component of the agency's Consumer Services Center. The official told us that the number of fraud operators at the Consumer Services Center had increased in the 1990's but has remained relatively constant at about 30 to 50 individuals since 1997. The official said that the cost of salaries for these operators has been approximately $900,000 per year, with annual adjustments to reflect inflation and merit increases. Also, the official noted that other administrative expenses—such as computer costs, rent payments, etc.—would raise the cost higher. However, the official did not quantify these expenses.

In describing Agency C's inquiry process, the official explained that consumers could place temporary or 6-month fraud alerts on their credit files by (1) using the agency's main automated toll free number and choosing the fraud option or (2) directly calling the fraud hotline and speaking with a fraud operator. According to this official:

- After temporary fraud alerts have been initiated, the consumers are automatically opted out of preapproved offers of credit.
- Additionally, the consumers receive free copies of their credit files. Upon reviewing their credit files, the consumers can contact a fraud operator and place a longer-term (2- to 7-year) fraud alert on their files.

CONSUMER CONFIDENCE IN ONLINE OR E-COMMERCE

The following sections present (1) overview information about Internet fraud, (2) credit industry views regarding identity theft and consumer confidence in using e-commerce, and (3) statistical data showing continued growth in e-commerce.

Overview: Internet Fraud

In addition to facilitating e-commerce, Internet technology can also increase the potential of exposing individuals to identity theft and other fraudulent activities or schemes. Generally, the term "Internet fraud" refers to any scheme that uses one or more components of the Internet—such as Web sites, message boards, e-mail, or chat rooms—to conduct fraudulent transactions, present fraudulent solicitations to prospective victims, or transmit the proceeds of fraud to financial institutions or others connected with the scheme. According to Internet Fraud Watch, which was created in 1996 to enable the National Fraud Information Center[33] to offer consumers advice about promotions in cyberspace and to route reports of suspected Internet and online fraud to the appropriate government agencies:

> "While scams online are both new and old, free standing and combinations, the Internet itself creates a whole new set of problems and opportunities for law enforcement and for criminals. There are millions of people online, with thousands of new users every day. … [T]here are now more e-mails sent every day than regular mail, including junk mail. Once a consumer goes online, he or she is bombarded with unsolicited commercial e-mail (spam) advertising everything from legitimate services to fraudulent investment schemes. Web sites abound offering both legitimate and fraudulent products and services."[34]

---

[33] The National Fraud Information Center was established in 1992 by the National Consumers League, a nonprofit consumer organization, to address telemarketing fraud by improving prevention and enforcement.

[34] Phillip C. McKee, III, Internet Fraud Watch Coordinator, "Remarks to the Annual Conference of the American Society of Travel Agents" (Oct. 8, 1999).

At a congressional hearing in September 2000, an FTC official testified, in part, as follows:

> "The Internet has dramatically altered the potential occurrence and impact of identity theft. First, the Internet provides access to identifying information through both illicit and legal means. The global publication of identifying details that previously were available only to a select few increases the potential for misuse of that information. Second, the ability of the identity thief to purchase goods and services from innumerable e-merchants expands the potential harm to the victim through numerous purchases. The explosion of financial services offered on-line, such as mortgages, credit cards, bank accounts and loans, provides a sense of anonymity to those potential identity thieves who would not risk committing identity theft in a face-to-face transaction."[35]

Recently, at a congressional hearing in May 2001, a Department of Justice official testified partly as follows:

> "Internet fraud, in all of its forms, is one of the fastest-growing and most pervasive forms of white-collar crime. ... Regrettably, criminal exploitation of the Internet now encompasses a wide variety of securities and other investment schemes, online auction schemes, credit-card fraud, financial institution fraud, and identity theft. ...
>
> "A January 2001 study by Meridien Research ... reports that with the continuing growth of e-commerce, payment-card fraud on the Internet will increase worldwide from $1.6 billion in 2000 to $15.5 billion by 2005. The Securities and Exchange Commission staff reports that it receives 200 to 300 online complaints a day about Internet-related securities fraud. Foreign law enforcement authorities also regard Internet fraud as a growing problem. Earlier this year, the European Commission reported that in 2000, payment-card fraud in the European Union rose by 50 percent to $553 million in fraudulent transactions, and noted that fraud was increasing most in relation to remote payment transactions, especially on the Internet. Similarly, the International Chamber of Commerce's Commercial Crime Service reported that nearly two-thirds of all cases it handled in 2000 involved online fraud."[36]

---

[35] FTC, prepared statement on Identity Theft for a hearing before the House Committee on Banking and Financial Services, (Sept. 13, 2000).

[36] Statement of Mr. Bruce Swartz, Deputy Assistant Attorney General, Criminal Division, Department of Justice, at a hearing ("On-line Fraud and Crime: Are Consumers Safe?") before the Subcommittee on Commerce, Trade, and Consumer Protection, House Committee on Energy and Commerce (May 23, 2001).

Industry Views: Payment Card Association and Selected Banks

At the May 2001 congressional hearing, a Senior Vice President from Visa—a major credit card association testified, in part, as follows:[37]

> "Electronic commerce is vital to the U.S. economy and to the prospects for our continued economic growth. ... There is no doubt that electronic commerce is a large, growing and permanent new channel for the sale of goods and services to consumers. The Department of Commerce estimates, for example, that online retail sales grew from less than $5.2 billion in the fourth quarter of 1999 to almost $8.7 billion in the same quarter one year later. Sales projections for the electronic commerce market range from $35 billion to $76 billion by the year 2002. By any measure, this counts as explosive growth ...
>
> "Visa has taken steps to promote consumer confidence in this new channel of commerce. These steps include ... [a] zero liability policy for unauthorized use of our payment cards. ... This zero liability policy applies to online transactions a well as offline transactions. Customers are protected online in exactly the same way as when they are using their cards at a store, ordering from a catalog by mail, or placing an order over the phone. In case of a problem, Visa provides 100 percent protection against unauthorized card use, theft, or loss. If someone steals a payment card number from one of our cardholders while the cardholder is shopping, online or offline, our customers are fully protected—they pay nothing for the thief's fraudulent activity."

During our review, of the six credit card-issuing banks we contacted, five responded to our questions about the impact of identity theft on consumer confidence in using e-commerce. These responses can be summarized as follows:

- One of the five banks had recently conducted a focus group to assess the issue of consumer confidence in using e-commerce. Bank officials told us that most of the focus group participants expressed no concern about identity theft or fraud in conducting online banking or e-commerce transactions. In the credit card issuer's experience, individuals over age 55 were more leery of online banking and e-commerce and were not as familiar with the technology.

- A second bank's officials told us that many of the bank's customers had an irrational fear of using e-commerce, or using credit cards for Internet transactions. The officials explained that, when fraud occurs, many customers were absolutely convinced the Internet was the root cause of the

---

[37] Statement of Mr. Mark MacCarthy, Senior Vice President, Public Policy, Visa U.S.A. Incorporated, at a hearing ("On-line Fraud and Crime: Are Consumers Safe?") before the Subcommittee on Commerce, Trade, and Consumer Protection, House Committee on Energy and Commerce (May 23, 2001).

compromised information and the subsequent fraud, regardless of whether or not the Internet was actually used in the fraudulent transaction.

- A third bank had conducted focus groups on fraud and found that the largest concern voiced was identity theft. However, according to bank officials, this concern was not a major barrier to using e-commerce.

- At the fourth and fifth banks, officials did not have any information about consumers' fears of identity theft from using online banking services or engaging in e-commerce transactions. However, officials from one of these banks noted that there was little basis in fact for such concerns. The officials explained that information transmitted to and from financial institutions for banking and other online transactions is encrypted; and, while there have been instances in which such information has been compromised, its misuse for identity theft purposes has been rare.

Steady Growth of E-Commerce

Despite concerns about security and privacy, the use of e-commerce by consumers has steadily grown. For example, in the 2000 holiday season, consumers spent an estimated $10.8 billion online, which represented more than a 50-percent increase over the $7 billion spent during the 1999 holiday season. Furthermore, in 1995, only 130 banks and thrifts had a Web site; but, the number had grown to 4,600 by 2000. Similarly, in 1995, only one bank had a Web site capable of processing financial transactions; but, by 2000, a total of 1,850 banks and thrifts had Web sites capable of processing financial transactions.[38]

The growth in e-commerce could indicate greater consumer confidence but could also result from the increasing number of people who have access to and are becoming familiar with Internet technology. According to an October 2000 Department of Commerce report, Internet users comprised about 44 percent (approximately 116 million people) of the U.S. population in August 2000. This was an increase of about 38 percent from 20 months prior.[39] According to Commerce's report, the fastest growing online activity among Internet users was online shopping and bill payment, which grew at a rate of 52 percent in 20 months. In short, as more consumers become familiar with online products and services, ecommerce is likely to

---

[38] Federal Deposit Insurance Corporation, *Evolving Financial Products, Services, and Delivery Systems* (Feb. 14, 2001).

[39] Department of Commerce, *Falling Through The Net: Toward Digital Inclusion* (Oct. 2000). This report was the fourth in a series of studies issued by Commerce on the technological growth of U.S. households and individuals.

gain greater acceptance as a channel of commerce, and usage can be expected to increase further.

APPENDIX III: COST OF IDENTITY THEFT TO VICTIMS

Victims of identity theft may experience a range of costs that encompass nonmonetary harm as well as monetary losses. This appendix presents information about both of these cost categories.

FTC Data on the Cost of Identity Theft to Victims

As mentioned previously, from its establishment in November 1999 through September 2001, the FTC Clearinghouse received a total of 94,100 complaints from identity theft victims. In response to our request, FTC staff provided us with information about the nonmonetary harm and the monetary losses (out-of-pocket expenses) reported by the complainants.

The extent of the harm reported to the FTC depends upon the victims' knowledge at the time that they call the FTC. Victims call the FTC at all stages of their experience with identity theft. Some victims call shortly after they discover the theft of their identities, while others may not hear about the FTC's hotline and not call until months after they discover the crime. In addition, some victims discover the misuse of their identity soon after the misuse begins, while others do not discover it until years later. Moreover, the thieves may continue to misuse identities long after victims contact the FTC. For these reasons, the amount of harm that the victims are aware of and report at the time that they call the FTC may not be the full extent of the harm they have experienced or will experience.

FTC Data on Nonmonetary Harm Reported by Identity Theft Complainants

As table 17 shows, of the 94,100 identity theft complaints reported to the FTC during November 1999 through September 2001, about 14 percent involved reports of nonmonetary harm. By far the most prevalent type of nonmonetary harm cited by consumers—mentioned in over 7,000 complaints—was "denied credit or other financial services." The second leading type of nonmonetary harm—cited in about 3,500 complaints—was "time lost to resolve problems." In nearly 1,300 complaints, identity theft victims alleged that they had been subjected to "criminal investigation, arrest, or conviction."

Table 17: Nonmonetary Harm Reported by Identity Theft Complainants to FTC (Nov. 1999 through Sept. 2001)

Nonmonetary harm	Number of complaints	Percent
Did the consumer report any nonmonetary harm?		
No	63,959	68.0
Information not collected (non-FTC data[a])	16,784	17.8
Yes	13,357	14.2
Totals	**94,100**	**100.0**
If yes, what was the harm?	Number of complaints	Percent based on subtotal[c]
Denied credit or other financial services[b]	7,376	55.2
Time lost to resolve problems	3,489	26.1
Harassed by debt collector or creditor	2,968	22.2
Criminal investigation, arrest, or conviction	1,281	9.6
Civil suit filed or judgment entered	819	6.1
Denied employment or loss of job	580	4.3
Other	3,780	28.3
Total	**13,357[d]**	

Note: According to FTC staff, most identity theft victims can be assumed to have received a negative or inaccurate credit report and, by itself, such a report is not a harm and is not included in this analysis. Rather, a negative or inaccurate credit report may result in various types of harm, such as the victim being denied credit, having to spend time to resolve problems, etc.

[a] Non-FTC data refer to identity theft complaints forwarded from the SSA/OIG to the FTC. In these complaints, information about nonmonetary harm to victims was not collected.

[b] Denied credit or other financial services includes being denied a loan, being denied a credit card, being denied a checking or savings account, having a credit card rejected, having a telephone or utilities cut off or new service denied, or having checks refused for payment (bounced).

[c] Percentages add to more than 100 percent because an identity theft complainant may allege more than one type of nonmonetary harm.

[d] Details add to more than 13,357 because an identity theft complainant may allege more than one type of nonmonetary harm.

Source: FTC data.

FTC Data on Monetary Losses Reported by Identity Theft Complainants

As table 18 shows, FTC data indicated that 2,633 complaints received from November 1999 through September 2001 involved dollar amounts that victims reported as having been lost or paid as out-of-pocket expenses as a result of identity theft. While most financial institutions do not hold victims liable for fraudulent debts, victims may incur significant expenses in trying to restore their good names and financial health. According to FTC staff, for example, victims routinely incur costs for document copies, notary fees, certified mail, and long-distance calls. Some consumers have tax refunds or other benefits withheld pending resolution of the identity theft crime. In addition, some consumers have hired attorneys. Other consumers reported that they chose to pay the fraudulent debt because of difficulties encountered in trying to have the debt absolved.

The FTC Clearinghouse had no data regarding direct out-of-pocket monetary losses (if any) for 77,063 (about 82 percent) of the 94,100 complaints received during November 1999 through September 2001. Also, for another 14,404 complaints, FTC data indicated that the individual victims reported zero dollar losses, that is, no out-of-pocket expenses. On the other hand, the data indicated that hundreds of complaints—2,633 in total during the 23-month period—reported at least some out-of-pocket expenses, with 207 of the complaints each alleging losses above $5,000 and another 203 complaints each alleging losses above $10,000. Out-of-pocket expenses may increase after victims report to the FTC and take further steps to resolve identity theft-related problems.

Table 18: Monetary Losses Reported by Identity Theft Complainants to FTC (Nov. 1999 through Sept. 2001)

Dollar amount of losses	Number of complaints	Percent
No data[a]	77,063	81.9
Zero dollar losses reported	14,404	15.3
Dollar losses reported:		
$1 – 100	502	0.5
$101 – 500	653	0.7
$501 – 1,000	399	0.4
$1,001 – 5,000	669	0.7
$5,001 – 10,000	207	0.2
Over $10,000	203	0.2
Subtotal	**2,633**	**2.8**
Total	**94,100**	**100.0**

[a] At the time they contacted the FTC, most complainants provided no information about the amount of out-of-pocket expenses, if any, they had incurred.

Source: FTC data.

Summary of Our Contacts with Victims

From its database of identity theft victims, after obtaining permission from the individuals, FTC staff provided us with the names and telephone numbers of 10 victims, whom we contacted to obtain a direct or first-hand understanding of their experiences. As presented in table 19:

Table 19: Summary of GAO's Interviews of Identity Theft Victims

Victim	For what fraudulent activities did the perpetrator use the victim's personal information?	What were the types of harm experienced by the victim?
1	Identity takeover activities: Opened 12 to 18 charge accounts. Obtained housing. Obtained utility services. Obtained fraudulent identification. Opened cellphone account.	Nonmonetary harm: Harassed by collection agency. Reappearance of charges after they had been removed. Expended time (about 200 hours over 10 months) to clear name. Monetary harm: Incurred out-of-pocket expenses ($100 to $200). Lost job and wages (about $6,000).
2	Identity takeover activities: Attempted to open charge account. Account takeover activities: Made charges on existing account.	Nonmonetary harm: Expended time (about 40 hours over 4 to 6 weeks) to clear name. Monetary harm: Incurred out-of-pocket expenses (less than $20).
3	Identity takeover activities: Opened charge accounts. Obtained housing. Purchased car. Wrote bad checks. Obtained employment and owed back taxes.	Nonmonetary harm: Expended time (about 3 months in worktime equivalent over 6 years) to clear name. Experienced difficulty obtaining credit. Monetary harm: Harassed by collection agencies. Incurred out-of-pocket expenses (about $20). Could not claim tax refund ($1,000).
4	Identity takeover activities: Opened charge accounts. Attempted to obtain car loan. Wrote bad checks. Obtained fraudulent identification. Opened cellphone account.	Nonmonetary harm: Expended time (between 150 and 200 hours over 6 weeks) to clear name. Monetary harm: Incurred out-of-pocket expenses (between $20 and $30 for notaries, faxes, etc.).
5	Identity takeover activities: Violated traffic laws (3 speeding tickets). Opened charge accounts. Wrote bad checks. Obtained employment and filed tax return. Obtained utility services. Obtained fraudulent identification. Attended college classes.	Nonmonetary harm: Arrest warrant issued for victim based on perpetrator's speeding tickets. Went to court to contest speeding ticket. Expended hundreds of hours over last 6 years. Experienced difficulty obtaining credit. Monetary harm: Could not obtain IRS tax refund ($814).
6	Identity takeover activities: Opened 10 charge accounts. Wrote bad checks. Made fraudulent identification. Account takeover activities: Used existing credit accounts.	Nonmonetary harm: Harassed by retailers over bad checks. Expended time (missed 3 days of work in 2 months). Had lower productivity at work. Monetary harm: Purse was stolen. Incurred out-of-pocket expenses for notaries and incidentals ($20).
7	Identity takeover activities: Opened about 20 charge accounts.	Nonmonetary harm: Experienced difficulty obtaining credit (rejected for credit 10 times).

Victim	For what fraudulent activities did the perpetrator use the victim's personal information?	What were the types of harm experienced by the victim?
		Expended time (about 48 hours over 2-½ years) to clear name. Experienced difficulty purchasing a car. Monetary harm: Incurred several hundred dollars in out-of-pocket expenses on notaries, faxes, etc.
8	Identity takeover activities: Filed for income tax refunds. Was arrested three times in victim's name.	Nonmonetary harm: Expended time (about 30 hours over 1-½ years) to clear name. Taken to police station for car to be searched for drugs.
9	Identity takeover activities: Obtained fraudulent identification. Opened bank account. Opened multiple charge accounts. Purchased car. Obtained prescription medication. Obtained employment and was fired from employment. Received unemployment benefits. Was evicted three times from housing. Used victim's name during auto accident. Was arrested twice in victim's name.	Nonmonetary harm: Experienced difficulty obtaining credit. Experienced difficulty obtaining employment. Experienced difficulty purchasing a car. Experienced difficulty obtaining housing due to perpetrator's eviction history. Expended hundreds of hours over 6 years attempting to clear name. Monetary harm: Lost job and wages ($2,500). Incurred out-of-pocket expenses (about $50).
10	Identity takeover activities: Obtained fraudulent identification. Opened multiple charge accounts. Received traffic violation in victim's name.	Nonmonetary harm: Experienced difficulty obtaining credit. Expended 15 to 20 hours over last 3 years attempting to clear name. Monetary harm: Incurred out-of-pocket expenses (about $59).

Note: According to FTC staff, the 10 victims were selected to illustrate a range in the number of types of identity theft activities reported by victims. The experiences of these 10 victims are not statistically representative of all identity theft victims.

Source: GAO's summary of telephone interviews with 10 identity theft victims FTC selected.

- In all 10 cases, the perpetrator used the victim's personal information to engage in identity takeover activities. Varying by case, such fraudulent activities ranged from the opening of new charge accounts and cellphone accounts to obtaining employment and filing tax returns in the victim's name. Also, in 2 of the 10 cases, the perpetrator engaged in account takeover activities; that is, the perpetrator made charges on existing accounts.

- Nine of the 10 victims reported experiencing both nonmonetary and monetary harms. Regarding nonmonetary harm, various victims reported being harassed by collection agencies, expending time to clear their names, having difficulty obtaining credit, and losing productivity at work.

Furthermore, one victim reportedly was the subject of an arrest warrant, based on speeding tickets issued to the perpetrator, and another victim was taken into police custody for a drug-related search stemming from the perpetrator's activities. Regarding monetary harm, the victims generally reported that out-of-pocket expenses were relatively low. However, two victims reported losing a job and wages (with losses of about $6,000 and $2,500 per victim, respectively), and two victims reported an inability to obtain tax refunds ($1,000 and $814, respectively).

In addition to the types of harm presented in table 19, several of the victims expressed to us feelings of "invaded privacy" and "continuing trauma" that likely would affect their lives for quite some time. In particular, such "lack of closure" was cited if elements of the crime involved more than one jurisdiction and/or if the victim had no awareness of any arrest being made. For instance, two victims reported being able to file a police report in their state of residence but were unable to do so in other states where the perpetrators committed fraudulent activities using the stolen identities. Also, 2 of the 10 victims told us they were aware that the perpetrator had been arrested.

Consumer Advocacy Report on the Cost of Identity Theft to Victims

In a May 2000 report, two nonprofit advocacy entities—the California Public Interest Research Group (CALPIRG) and the Privacy Rights Clearinghouse—presented findings based on a survey (conducted in the spring of 2000) of 66 identity theft victims who had contacted these organizations.[40] The May 2000 report noted that victims of identity theft "face extreme difficulties attempting to clear the damaged credit, or even criminal record, caused by the thief." According to the report, the following findings illustrate the obstacles that victims encounter when trying to resolve their identity theft cases:

- The victims spent 175 hours, on average, actively trying to resolve their identity theft-related problems. Less than half (45 percent) of the respondents believed that their cases had been fully resolved; these respondents reported an average of 23 months to reach resolution. The other survey respondents (55 percent) reported that their unresolved cases had already been open, on average, for 44 months.

---

[40] CALPIRG (Sacramento, Cal. and Privacy Rights Clearinghouse (San Diego, Cal., "Nowhere to Turn: Victims Speak Out on Identity Theft" (May 2000).

- Not counting legal fees, victims reported spending between $30 and $2,000 on costs related to their identity theft. The average reported loss was $808, but most victims estimated spending $100 for out-of-pocket costs.

- The majority (76 percent) of the surveyed cases involved "true name fraud"—which occurred, for instance, when the imposter opened new credit accounts in the name of the victim. The number of fraudulent new accounts opened per victim ranged from 1 to 30, and the average was 6 new accounts.

The May 2000 report stated that these findings may not be representative of the plight of all victims. Rather, the report noted that the findings should be viewed as "preliminary and representative only of those victims who have contacted our organizations for further assistance (other victims may have had simpler cases resolved with only a few calls and felt no need to make further inquiries)."

Later, at a national conference, the Director of Privacy Rights Clearinghouse expanded on the results of the May 2000 report. For instance, regarding the 66 victims surveyed, the Director noted that one in six (about 15 percent) said that they had been the subject of a criminal record because of the actions of an imposter.[41] Furthermore, the Director provided additional comments substantially as follows:

- Unlike checking for credit report inaccuracies, there is no easy way for consumers to determine if they have become the subject of a criminal record.

- Indeed, victims of identity theft may not discover that they have been burdened with a criminal record until, for example, they are stopped for a traffic violation and are then arrested because the officer's checking of the driver's license number indicated that an arrest warrant was outstanding.

Additional Observations

In an April 2001 advisory letter to national banks, the Office of the Comptroller of the Currency (OCC) made the following observations about the cost of identity theft:

> "This growing crime has a devastating effect on financial institution customers and a detrimental impact on the banks. Four of the top five consumer complaints regarding identity theft involve financial services—new credit card accounts opened, existing credit card accounts used, new deposit accounts opened, and newly obtained loans.

---

[41] Beth Givens, Director, Privacy Rights Clearinghouse, "Identity theft: The Growing Problem of Wrongful Criminal Records," presented at the SEARCH National Conference on Privacy, Technology and Criminal Justice Information, in Washington, D.C. (June 1, 2000).

Banks absorb much of the economic losses from bank fraud associated with the theft of their customers' identities. Individuals who become victims of identity theft also pay, at a minimum, out-of-pocket expenses to clear their names and may spend numerous hours trying to rectify their credit records."[42]

Also, in congressional testimony in May 2001, an experienced New York City police detective characterized the cost of identity theft to victims as follows:

"Over the past five years, there has been a significant increase in crimes where criminals compromise personal identification data of victims, in order to commit identity theft. The information that falls into criminal hands includes name, date of birth, Social Security Number, banking account number, and other personal and financial information.

"Victims of identity theft, like other crime victims, are made to feel personally violated. This is especially true in light of the vicious cycle of event that typically follows the perpetration of this crime. Imagine for a moment, a recently married couple just starting out in their life together. They work hard and save enough money to make a down payment on their first new home only to be denied a mortgage because of a negative payment history reflected in a credit report—information that they knew nothing about. The trauma of this type of fraud causes its innocent victims is unimaginable. Moreover, once the crime is discovered and reported, victims are left to fend for themselves in attempting to clear their credit history and good name.

"Our unit has successfully conducted numerous investigations where perpetrators have used the personal information to not only obtain credit cards and personal loans, but also to purchase cars and homes. Although we in law enforcement garner some sense of satisfaction when we make arrests for these crimes, it is not enough when compared to the amount of time and energy a victim spends trying to undo the work of these criminals."[43]

APPENDIX IV: COST OF IDENTITY THEFT TO THE FEDERAL CRIMINAL JUSTICE SYSTEM

This appendix presents information about the cost of identity theft to the federal criminal justice system—that is, the cost associated with investigations, prosecutions, incarceration, and community supervision. Generally, we found that federal agencies do not separately maintain statistics on the person hours, portions of salary, or other

---

[42] Comptroller of the Currency, Administrator of National Banks, OCC Advisory Letter (AL 2001-4), Subject: Identity Theft and Pretext Calling (Apr. 30, 2001), pp. 2-3.

[43] Testimony of Detective Michael Fabozzi, New York City Police Department, hearing on "Protecting Privacy and Preventing Misuse of Social Security Numbers" before the Subcommittee on Social Security, House Committee on Ways and Means (May 22, 2001).

distinct costs that are specifically attributable to cases involving 18 U.S.C. §1028(a)(7) and other criminal statutes that may be applicable to identity theft and fraud. Thus, as an alternative, some of the agencies provided us with average cost estimates based, for example, on white-collar crime cases—a category that covers financial crimes, including identity theft.

Cost of Investigations

Various Justice Department law enforcement agencies (e.g., the FBI), Treasury Department agencies (e.g., the Secret Service), and the Postal Inspection Service are responsible for investigating possible federal criminal violations in which identity theft or fraud is a factor. Also, the SSA's Office of the Inspector General (OIG) may investigate possible identity theft and fraud cases where misuse or abuse of Social Security numbers (SSNs) is involved. Three of these agencies—the FBI, the Secret Service, and SSA/OIG—responded to our request for cost-related information, as discussed in the following sections.

FBI: Cost of Investigations

In response to our inquiry regarding the cost of investigating identity theft crimes, the FBI provided us with an estimate based on budget and workload data for the agency's white-collar crime program for fiscal years 1998 to 2000. For this 3-year period, the FBI estimated that approximately $20,000 was the average cost of an investigative matter handled by the agency's white-collar crime program. However, an FBI official noted that the agency does not have cost data related specifically to identity theft cases, and the official told us that the average-cost figure ($20,000) was not very meaningful given the following caveats:

- Using available data, the average cost of an investigative matter can be calculated in a number of different ways, none of which is perfect. Due to such imperfections, the validity of the $20,000 figure is highly questionable. For instance, the average cost figure does not capture the wide variance in the scope and costs of white-collar crime investigations. Some cases can be of short duration and involve only one FBI agent, whereas other cases can be very complicated, be ongoing for several years, and involve many agents.

- Also, it is questionable methodology for the FBI to apply the average cost of its white-collar crime investigations in general to identity theft cases specifically. Identity theft is rarely a stand-alone crime; that is, identity theft is frequently an element of bank fraud, wire fraud, and other types of white-collar or financial crimes. On the other hand, some white-collar or financial crimes, including some high-cost cases, may not involve elements of identity theft. However, the FBI's information systems are not sufficiently code to isolate identity theft-related budget and workload data within the white-collar crime program.

Secret Service: Cost of Investigations

We asked the Secret Service for an estimate of the average cost of investigating financial crimes that included identity theft as a component. The Secret Service responded that the agency does not track costs on a per-case basis and noted that the nature and variety of factors regularly present in common investigative scenarios do not lend themselves to accurate "average cost" tracking. The agency explained that variants affecting cost include, but are not limited to, the number of personnel assigned, the use of technical and surveillance assets, transcription and translation services, case-related travel (domestic and foreign), task force expenses, expenditures for investigative information and evidence, expenditures associated with undercover activities, and trial preparation. In summary, the Secret Service responded that its cases vary so much in their makeup that to put a figure on average cost is not meaningful.

Nonetheless, recognizing these caveats, the Secret Service's Management and Organization Division made its "best estimate of the average cost" of a financial crimes investigation conducted by the Secret Service in fiscal year 2001. The resulting estimate was approximately $15,000. Secret Service officials noted that this estimate was for a financial crimes investigation and not specifically for an identity theft investigation. Also, the officials emphasized that, in the absence of specific guidelines establishing a standard methodology, average-cost figures provide no basis for making interagency comparisons.

SSA/OIG: No Estimate of Cost

We asked SSA/OIG for an estimate of the average cost of investigating cases involving SSN misuse. SSA/OIG officials responded that the agency's information systems do not record time spent by function to permit making an accurate estimate of what it costs to work these types of cases. Furthermore, the officials commented substantially as follows:

- Identity theft poses greater costs to the public and to financial institutions than to law enforcement.

- The cost of identity theft to law enforcement is a moving target. The cost can be small or large, depending on what priority SSN misuse is given in any law enforcement organization.

- In fact, SSA/OIG probably could dedicate its entire workforce to SSN misuse cases and still not scrape the surface of this issue.

Finally, the SSA/OIG officials noted that the SSA/OIG's appropriations for fiscal year 2001 totaled about $69 million; however, the officials reiterated the impracticality of estimating how much of this amount was used for investigating cases of SSN misuse.

Cost of Prosecutions

Executive Office for U.S. Attorneys (EOUSA) officials said that the agency's timekeeping system could not specifically isolate the cost of prosecuting identity theft cases. The officials noted, however, that such cases generally are categorized as white-collar crimes, as are other types of financial crimes. According to EOUSA:

- U.S. Attorney Offices handled a total of 13,720 white-collar crime cases in fiscal year 2000. This total includes all white-collar crime cases that U.S. Attorney Offices dealt with in any manner during the year. That is, the total includes cases that were closed in the year, cases that were opened in the year, and cases that were still pending at year end.

- The total cost associated with the 13,720 white-collar crime cases handled was $157 million in fiscal year 2000. Thus, the estimated average annual cost of prosecuting a white-collar crime case was $11,443.

EOUSA emphasized that this figure was derived using a broad, inexact methodology. Furthermore, EOUSA emphasized that the figure was only an estimate and that the actual cost could be higher or lower.

Cost of Incarceration

According to Bureau of Prisons (BOP) officials, federal offenders convicted of white-collar crimes generally are incarcerated in minimum-security correctional facilities. For fiscal year 2000, BOP officials told us that the cost of operating such facilities averaged $47.68 daily per inmate. Thus, on a monthly (30 days per month) and an annual basis (365 days per year), the respective cost figures would be $1,430 per inmate and $17,403 per inmate.

Cost of Community Supervision

Federal probation officers are responsible for the community supervision of federal offenders released from prison, as well as those placed on probation in lieu of a prison sentence. Each offender under supervision is assigned to a designated probation officer, whose responsibilities include (1) enforcing the conditions of supervision; (2) reducing the risk the offender poses to the community; and (3) providing the offender with access to treatment, such as substance abuse aftercare and mental health services.[44] Offenders are typically supervised in the community for a period of 3 to 5 years.

In response to our inquiry, AOUSC provided us average daily cost data covering all federal offenders under supervision. The average daily cost reported for fiscal year 2000 ranged from $8.02 for regular supervision to $31.46 for supervision that involved electronic monitoring and substance abuse treatment. An AOUSC official told us that white-collar offenders—including those who committed identity theft and do not need contract services—probably would fall into the regular supervision category. For this category, the average daily cost of $8.02 equates to about $2,900 annually per offender. According to AOUSC, regular supervision cost is based on the national average salary and benefits of a U.S. probation officer, plus additional costs associated with management, administrative support, training, and overhead (e.g., automation, space, telephone service, and travel).

---

[44] Title 18, section 3583 of the U.S. Code provides for inclusion of a term of supervised release after imprisonment. Section 3603 specifies the duties of probation officers.

Chapter 3

REMEDIES AVAILABLE TO VICTIMS OF IDENTITY THEFT[†]

Angie A. Welborn

INTRODUCTION

According to the Federal Trade Commission, identity theft is the most common complaint from consumers in all fifty states, and complaints regarding identity theft have grown for three consecutive years.[1] Victims of identity theft may incur damaged credit records, unauthorized charges on credit cards, and unauthorized withdrawals from bank accounts. Sometimes, victims must change their telephone numbers or even their Social Security numbers. Victims may also need to change addresses that were falsified by the impostor.

This chapter provides an overview of the federal laws that could assist victims of identity theft with purging inaccurate information from their credit records and removing unauthorized charges from credit accounts, as well as federal laws that impose criminal penalties on those who assume another person's identity through the use of fraudulent identification documents. State laws and recent legislative proposals (S. 22, S. 153, S. 223, S. 228, S. 745, H.R. 220, H.R. 637, H.R. 818, H.R. 858, H.R. 1636, H.R. 1729, H.R. 1731, H.R. 1931, H.R. 2035, 2617, H.R. 2622, and H.R. 2633) aimed at preventing identity theft and providing additional remedies are also discussed.

[†] Excerpted from CRS Report RL31919. Updated July 9, 2003.
[1] [http://www.consumer.gov/sentinel/trends.htm].

FEDERAL STATUTES RELATED TO IDENTITY THEFT

Identity Theft Assumption and Deterrence Act

While not exclusively aimed at consumer identity theft, the Identity Theft Assumption Deterrence Act prohibits fraud in connection with identification documents under a variety of circumstances.[2] Certain offenses under the statute relate directly to consumer identity theft, and impostors could be prosecuted under the statute. For example, the statute makes it a federal crime, under certain circumstances,[3] to knowingly and without lawful authority produce an identification document[4] or false identification document; or to knowingly possess an identification document that is or appears to be an identification document of the United States which is stolen or produced without lawful authority knowing that such document was stolen or produced without such authority.[5] It is also a federal crime to knowingly transfer or use, without lawful authority, a means of identification of another person with the intent to commit, or aid or abet, any unlawful activity that constitutes a violation of federal law, or that constitutes a felony under any applicable state or local law.[6]

The punishment for offenses involving fraud related to identification documents varies depending on the specific offense and the type of document involved.[7] For example, a fine or imprisonment of up to 15 years may be imposed for using the identification of another person with the intent to commit any unlawful activity under state law, if, as a result of the offense, the person committing the offense obtains

---

[2] 18 U.S.C. 1028. The statute lists several actions that constitute fraud in connection with identification documents. However, for the purposes of this report, they do not all relate to consumer-related identity theft, i.e. situations where a consumer's Social Security number or driver's license number may be stolen and used to establish credit accounts by an impostor.

[3] According to the statute, the prohibitions listed apply when "the identification document or false identification document is or appears to be issued by or under the authority of the United States or the document-making implement is designed or suited for making such an identification document or false identification document;" the document is presented with the intent to defraud the United States; or "either the production, transfer, possession, or use prohibited by this section is in or affects interstate or foreign commerce, including the transfer of a document by electronic means, or the means of identification, identification document, false identification document, or document-making implement is transported in the mail in the course of the production, transfer, possession, or use prohibited by this section." 18 U.S.C. 1028(c).

[4] Identification document is defined as "a document made or issued by or under the authority of the United States Government, a State, political subdivision of a State, a foreign government, political subdivision of a foreign government, an international governmental or an internal quasi-governmental organization which, when completed with information concerning a particular individual, is of a type intended or commonly accepted for the purpose of identification of individuals." 18 U.S.C. 1028(d)(2). Identification documents include Social Security cards, birth certificates, driver's licenses, and personal identification cards.

[5] 18 U.S.C. 1028(a)(1) and (2).

[6] 18 U.S.C. 1028(a)(7).

[7] 18 U.S.C. 1028(b).

anything of value totaling $1,000 or more during any one-year period.[8] Other offenses carry terms of imprisonment up to three years.[9] However, if the offense is committed to facilitate a drug trafficking crime or in connection with a crime of violence, the term of imprisonment could be up to twenty years.[10] Offenses committed to facilitate an action of international terrorism are punishable by terms of imprisonment up to twenty-five years.[11]

Fair Credit Reporting Act

While the Fair Credit Reporting Act (FCRA) does not directly address identity theft, it could offer victims assistance in having negative information resulting from unauthorized charges or accounts removed from their credit files. The purpose of the FCRA is "to require that consumer reporting agencies adopt reasonable procedures for meeting the needs of commerce for consumer credit, personnel, insurance, and other information in a manner which is fair and equitable to the consumer, with regard to the confidentiality, accuracy, relevancy, and proper utilization of such information."[12] The FCRA outlines a consumer's rights in relation to his or her credit report, as well as permissible uses for credit reports and disclosure requirements. In addition, the FCRA requires credit reporting agencies to follow "reasonable procedures to assure maximum possible accuracy of the information concerning the individual about whom the report relates."[13]

The FCRA allows consumers to file suit for violations of the Act, which could include the disclosure of inaccurate information about a consumer by a credit reporting agency.[14] A consumer who is a victim of identity theft could file suit against a credit reporting agency for the agency's failure to verify the accuracy of information contained in the report and the agency's disclosure of inaccurate information as a result of the consumer's stolen identity. Generally, the FCRA requires a consumer to file suit "within two years from the date on which the liability arises."[15] However, there is an exception in cases where there was willful misrepresentation of information that is required to be disclosed to a consumer and such information is material to the establishment of the defendant's liability.[16] In such cases, the action

---

[8] 18 U.S.C. 1028(b)(1)(D).
[9] 18 U.S.C. 1028(b)(2).
[10] 18 U.S.C. 1028(b)(3).
[11] 18 U.S.C. 1028(b)(4).
[12] 15 U.S.C. 1681(b).
[13] 15 U.S.C. 1681e(b).
[14] 15 U.S.C. 1681n; 15 U.S.C. 1681o. For more information see CRS Report RS21083, *Identity Theft and the Fair Credit Reporting Act: An Analysis of* TRW v. Andrews *and Current Legislation.*
[15] 15 U.S.C. 1681p.
[16] *Id.*

"may be brought any time within two years after the discovery by the individual of the misrepresentation."[17]

Fair Credit Billing Act

The Fair Credit Billing Act (FCBA) is not an identity theft statute *per se*, but it does provide consumers with an opportunity to receive an explanation and proof of charges that may have been made by an impostor and to have unauthorized charges removed from their accounts. The purpose of the FCBA is "to protect the consumer against inaccurate and unfair credit billing and credit card practices."[18] The law defines and establishes a procedure for resolving billing errors in consumer credit transactions. For purposes of the FCBA, a "billing error" includes unauthorized charges, charges for goods or services not accepted by the consumer or delivered to the consumer, and charges for which the consumer has asked for an explanation or written proof of purchase.[19]

Under the FCBA, consumers are able to file a claim with the creditor to have billing errors resolved. Until the alleged billing error is resolved, the consumer is not required to pay the disputed amount, and the creditor may not attempt to collect, any part of the disputed amount, including related finance charges or other charges.[20] The Act sets forth dispute resolution procedures and requires an investigation into the consumer's claims. If the creditor determines that the alleged billing error did occur, the creditor is obligated to correct the billing error and credit the consumer's account with the disputed amount and any applicable finance charges.[21]

Electronic Fund Transfer Act

Similar to the Fair Credit Billing Act, the Electronic Fund Transfer Act is not an identity theft statute *per se*, but it does provide consumers with a mechanism for challenging unauthorized transactions and having their accounts recredited in the event of an error. The purpose of the Electronic Fund Transfer Act (EFTA) is to "provide a basic framework establishing the rights, liabilities, and responsibilities of participants in electronic fund transfer systems."[22] Among other things, the EFTA limits a consumer's liability for unauthorized electronic fund transfers. If the consumer notifies the financial institution within two business days after learning of

---

[17] *Id.*
[18] 15 U.S.C. 1601(a).
[19] 15 U.S.C. 1666(b); 12 C.F.R. 226.13(a).
[20] 15 U.S.C. 1666(c); 12 C.F.R. 226.13(d)(1).
[21] 15 U.S.C. 1666(a); 12 C.F.R. 226.13(e).
[22] 15 U.S.C. 1693(b).

the loss or theft of a debit card or other device used to make electronic transfers, the consumer's liability is limited to the lesser of $50 or the amount of the unauthorized transfers that occurred before notice was given to the financial institution.[23]

Additionally, financial institutions are required to provide a consumer with documentation of all electronic fund transfers initiated by the consumer from an electronic terminal. If a financial institution receives, within 60 days after providing such documentation, an oral or written notice from the consumer indicating the consumer's belief that the documentation provided contains an error, the financial institution must investigate the alleged error, determine whether an error has occurred, and report or mail the results of the investigation and determination to the consumer within ten business days.[24] The notice from the consumer to the financial institution must identify the name and account number of the consumer; indicate the consumer's belief that the documentation contains an error and the amount of the error; and set forth the reasons for the consumer's belief that an error has occurred.[25]

In the event that the financial institution determines that an error has occurred, the financial institution must correct the error within one day of the determination in accordance with the provisions relating to the consumer's liability for unauthorized charges.[26] The financial institution may provisionally recredit the consumer's account for the amount alleged to be in error pending the conclusion of its investigation and its determination of whether an error has occurred, if it is unable to complete the investigation within ten business days.[27]

STATE IDENTITY THEFT STATUTES

State Criminal Laws

Most states have enacted some type of criminal identity theft statute.[28] Many of these statutes impose criminal monetary penalties for identity theft activities. For example, in California, impostors are subject to fines of up to $10,000 and confinement in jail for up to one year.[29] Restitution may also be a component of the impostor's punishment. In Texas, identity theft is a felony and, in addition to jail time, the court may order the impostor to reimburse the victim for lost income and other expenses incurred as a result of the theft.[30] Other states impose civil penalties and

---

[23] 15 U.S.C. 1693g(a), 12 C.F.R. 205.6(b)(1).
[24] 15 U.S.C. 1693f(a), 12 C.F.R. 205.11(b) and (c).
[25] Id.
[26] 15 U.S.C. 1693f(b).
[27] 15 U.S.C. 1693f(c), 12 C.F.R. 205.11(c).
[28] For a list of state identity theft statutes see [http://www.consumer.gov/idtheft/statelaw.htm].
[29] Cal. Penal Code §§ 530.5 - 530.7.
[30] Tex. Penal Code § 32.51. *See also* Va. Code Ann. § 18.2-186.3; Md. Code Ann. art. 27 § 231.

provide victims with judicial recourse for damages incurred as a result of the theft. In Washington, impostors are "liable for civil damages of five hundred dollars or actual damages, whichever is greater, including costs to repair the victim's credit record."[31]

While some statutes may define identity theft to include only the fraudulent use of identification documents, other statutes may more broadly define such activities. For example, Oregon also criminalizes the fraudulent use of credit cards. Such use constitutes a felony if the "aggregate total amount of property or services the person obtains or attempts to obtain is $750 or more."[32] In Illinois, the crime of financial identity theft includes the fraudulent use of credit card numbers, in addition to the fraudulent use of identification documents.[33]

State Laws Aimed at Assisting Victims

In addition to the states that provide for criminal prosecution of impostors, some states have enacted laws aimed at assisting victims of identity theft. At least three states – California, Idaho, and Washington – have enacted laws allowing victims of identity theft to place fraud alerts on their credit reports or have information resulting from the alleged theft blocked from their credit reports.[34]

California has enacted what some consider to be the most extensive law aimed at assisting victims of identity theft and preventing future occurrences. Under California law, a consumer may request that a security alert be placed in his or her credit report to notify recipients of the report "that the consumer's identity may have been used without the consumer's consent to fraudulently obtain goods or services in the consumer's name."[35] Consumer reporting agencies are required to notify each person requesting consumer credit information with respect to a consumer of the existence of a security alert in the consumer's report, regardless of whether a full credit report, credit score, or summary report is requested.[36]

A consumer may also be able to have a security freeze placed on his or her credit report by making a request in writing by certified mail with a consumer credit reporting agency.[37] A security freeze prohibits the consumer reporting agency from releasing the consumer's credit report or any information from it without the express authorization of the consumer.[38] The consumer reporting agency may advise a third party requesting the consumer's report that a security freeze is in place, but may not

---

[31] RCW 9.35.020(3).
[32] Or. Rev. Stat. § 165.055.
[33] 720 ILCS 5/16G-10. *See also* Ohio Rev. Code Ann. § 2913.49.
[34] California, Cal. Civ. Code § 1785.11.1; Idaho, Idaho Code § 28-51-02; Washington, RCW 19.182.160.
[35] Cal. Civ. Code § 1785.11.1(a).
[36] Cal. Civ. Code § 1785.11.1(b).
[37] Cal. Civ. Code § 1785.11.2(a).
[38] *Id.*

release any additional information without prior express authorization from the consumer. If a security freeze is in place, a consumer credit reporting agency may not change the name, date of birth, social security number, or address in a consumer credit report without sending a written confirmation of the change to the consumer within 30 days of the change being posted to the consumer's file.[39] In the case of an address change, the written confirmation must be sent to both the new address and to the former address.

Victims of identity theft who are sued on an obligation resulting from the theft, may bring a cross-claim alleging identity theft. If the victim prevails, he or she is entitled to a judgment stating that he or she is not responsible for the debt or other basis for the claim and an injunction restraining any collection efforts.[40] The victim may join other claimants, and the court may keep jurisdiction for up to ten years, so as to resolve all claims resulting from the theft.

A new provision which became effective July 1, 2003, requires a consumer reporting agency to provide consumers who have reason to believe that they are victims of identity theft with information as to their rights under California law.[41] Upon receipt from a victim of identity theft of a police report or a valid investigative report, a consumer reporting agency must also provide a victim of identity theft with up to 12 copies of his or her credit report during a consecutive 12-month period free of charge.[42]

Washington has also enacted an extensive identity theft statute that includes provisions aimed at assisting victims of identity theft. As noted above, the Washington identity theft statute has a provision that allows consumers to block information resulting from identity theft from their credit reports. A consumer reporting agency must block such information within 30 days of receiving a copy of a police report regarding the alleged theft.[43] Another provision allows victims of identity theft to receive information about the alleged crime from persons who may have entered into transactions with the impostor. Upon the request of the victim, such persons must provide copies of all relevant application and transaction information related to the alleged fraudulent transaction.[44]

---

[39] Cal. Civ. Code § 1785.11.3(a).
[40] Cal. Civ. Code § 1798.2.
[41] Cal. Civ. Code § 1785.15.3(a).
[42] Cal. Civ. Code § 1785.15.3(b).
[43] RCW 19.182.160.
[44] RCW 9.35.040.

LEGISLATIVE PROPOSALS

107th Congress

During the 107th Congress, numerous bills related to identity theft were introduced.

108th Congress

To date, a number of bills related to identity theft have been introduced in the 108th Congress. With the exception of S. 153, which was passed by the Senate, without amendment, on March 19, no additional action has been taken on this legislation, though both the House and the Senate have held hearings on identity theft and financial privacy. In general, these bills include provisions similar to those found in legislation introduced during the 107th Congress.

Title III of **S. 22**, the **Justice Enhancement and Domestic Security Act of 2003**, includes several provisions aimed at deterring and preventing identity theft, including identity theft mitigation, amendments to the Fair Credit Reporting Act requiring the blocking of information on a consumer's credit report resulting from identity theft, an amendment to the FCRA's statute of limitations, provisions related to the misuse of social security numbers, and prevention provisions similar to those in S. 223 discussed below.

S. 153, the **Identity Theft Penalty Enhancement Act**, would amend Title 18 of the United States Code to establish penalties for aggravated identity theft and make changes to the existing identity theft provisions of Title 18. Under S. 153, aggravated identity theft would occur when a person "knowingly transfers, possess, or uses, without lawful authority, a means of identification of another person" during and in relation to the commission of certain enumerated felonies. The penalty for aggravated identity theft would be a term of imprisonment of 2 years in addition to the punishment provided for the original felony committed. Offenses committed in conjunction with certain terrorism offenses would be subject to an additional term of imprisonment of 5 years. **H.R. 858** and **H.R. 1731** appear to be substantially similar.

S. 223, the **Identity Theft Prevention Act**, includes several provisions aimed at preventing identity theft, including a requirement that credit card issuers confirm change of address requests, a requirement that consumer reporting agencies include fraud alerts in consumer reports at the request of the consumer, and a requirement that credit card numbers on printed receipts be truncated.

S. 228, the **Social Security Number Misuse Prevention Act**, would prohibit the display, sale, or purchase of an individual's social security number with limited exceptions. It would also prohibit the display, sale, or purchase of public records containing social security numbers, and prohibit the use of social security numbers on certain government documents, such as checks and driver's licenses. The bill would also place limitations on the use of social security numbers by commercial entities. **H.R. 637** appears to be substantially similar.

S. 745, the **Privacy Act of 2003**, while not directly related to identity theft, includes numerous provisions aimed at protecting the privacy of personal information, which could assist identity theft prevention efforts. Provisions set forth in S. 745 would generally prohibit the collection and distribution of personally identifiable information unless the individual receives notification and is provided an opportunity to restrict the disclosure or sale of such information; prohibit the display, sale, or purchase of an individual's Social Security number without consent from the individual; place limitations on the sale and sharing of nonpublic personal financial information; place limitations on the provisions of protected health information; and prohibit the release of certain information included on an individual's driver's license.

H.R. 220, the **Identity Theft Prevention Act of 2003**, would place new restrictions on the use of social security numbers and require all social security numbers to be randomly generated.

H.R. 818, the **Identity Theft Consumer Notification Act**, would require financial institutions to notify consumers whose personal information has been compromised. The financial institution would also be required to assist the individual by correcting information in the consumer's credit file and to compensate the consumer for any monetary losses resulting from the compromise. The bill would also amend the Fair Credit Reporting Act's statute of limitations to allow additional time for a consumer to file suit.

H.R. 1636, the **Consumer Privacy Protection Act of 2003**, includes several provisions aimed at protecting consumer privacy. Title I of the bill addresses a consumer's rights with respect to the use or dissemination of his or her personal information in interstate commerce, including a requirement that consumers be given an opportunity to preclude the sale or disclosure of the consumer's personally identifiable information. Title II specifically addresses the prevention of identity theft and provides remedies for victims of identity theft. The bill would require the Federal Trade Commission to take actions necessary to permit consumers to file electronic identity theft affidavits with the Commission and to promote the use of a common identity theft affidavit among entities that receive disputes regarding the unauthorized use of accounts from consumers that have reason to believe that they are victims of identity theft. The legislation also directs the FTC to require such entities to resolve identity theft disputes within 90 days from the date on which all necessary information to investigate the claim has been submitted. The bill would also make improvements to the Commission's consumer clearinghouse, and require the collection of data from public and private entities that receive and process complaints from consumers that have a reasonable belief that they are victims of identity theft.

H.R. 1729, the **Negative Credit Notification Act**, would require a consumer reporting agency to notify a consumer if any information that is, or may be construed as being, adverse to the interests of the consumer is added to the consumer's file. The notification must also include a brief description of the information "sufficient to allow the consumer to determine the accuracy or completeness of the information so furnished and the source of the information."

H.R. 1931, the **Personal Information Privacy Act of 2003**, includes several provisions aimed at protecting an individual's Social Security number and other personal information. The bill would amend the Fair Credit Reporting Act to include in the definition of a consumer report any identifying information of the consumer, except the name, address and telephone number of the consumer if listed in a residential telephone directory available in the locality of the consumer, and require a consumer reporting agency to receive express written authorization from a consumer prior to releasing information with respect to a transaction that was not initiated by the consumer. An additional amendment to the FCRA would add a new section prohibiting the sale or transfer of transaction or experience information without the consumer's express written consent. H.R. 1931 would also prohibit the use of an individual's Social Security number for commercial purposes without consent.

H.R. 2035, the **Identity Theft and Financial Privacy Act of 2003**, includes several provisions aimed at preventing identity theft. The bill would require credit card issuers to confirm change of address requests if such request is received within 30 days of a request for an additional card, and amend the Fair Credit Reporting Act to require consumer reporting agencies to notify requesters of potential fraud when the request includes an address for the consumer that is substantially different from the most recent address on file with the consumer reporting agency. An additional amendment to the FCRA would require consumer reporting agencies, upon receipt of proper identification, to include a fraud alert in a consumer's file if the consumer has been or suspects that he or she is about to become a victim of identity theft. The consumer reporting agency would be required to notify each person procuring the consumer's file of the existence of a fraud alert, regardless of whether a full credit report, credit score, or summary report is requested. The Federal Trade Commission would be required to promulgate rules providing for procedures for referral of consumer complaints about identity theft and fraud alters between and among the consumer reporting agencies and the Commission. In addition, rules developing a model form and standard procedures to be used by consumers who are victims of identity theft for contacting and informing creditors and consumer agencies of the fraud would be required. H.R. 2035 would also require the truncation of credit card numbers on printed receipts and require consumer reporting agencies to provide free credit reports annually upon the request of a consumer.

H.R. 2617, the **Consumer Identity and Information Security Act of 2003**, includes several provisions aimed at preventing identity theft and assisting victims.

The bill would prohibit certain actions with respect to an individual's social security number, including prohibitions on the display of an individual's social security number and a prohibition on requiring an individual to transmit his or her social security number over the Internet. The truncation of credit and debit card numbers on receipts would also be required. The bill would also require credit card issuers to verify a consumer's identity if the issuer receives a change of address request within 30 days of receiving a request for an additional card. Consumer reporting agencies would also be required, upon receipt of proper identification, to include in a consumer's file a fraud alert and notify all subsequent users of the consumer's report of the existence of the alert. A consumer reporting agency that maintains files on a nationwide basis would be required to notify other such agencies of the alert, and such agencies would then be required to place similar alerts in the files they maintain.

H.R. 2622, the **Fair and Accurate Credit Transactions Act of 2003**, includes, *inter alia*, several provisions aimed at preventing identity theft and assisting victims of identity theft. The bill would amend the Fair Credit Reporting Act to require credit card issuers to investigate change of address requests if the issuer receives a request for an additional credit card within 30 days of receiving notification of a change of address. Another amendment to the FCRA would require consumer reporting agencies to include fraud alerts in a consumer's file upon the request of the consumer. Once included, the agency would be required to notify each person procuring the report of the existence of the alert, and users of the report would be required to attempt to obtain the authorization or preauthorization of the consumer prior to issuing or extending credit in the name of the consumer to a person other than the consumer. The bill would also require the truncation of credit card and debit card account numbers.

Provisions aimed at assisting victims include an amendment to the FCRA which would require consumer reporting agencies to develop procedures for providing consumers who believe that they have been a victim of identity theft with a summary of the rights of consumers under the Consumer Credit Protection Act and other provisions of federal law that may help remedy the effects of the alleged offense. An additional amendment to the FCRA would require consumer reporting agencies, after receipt of proof of identity of the consumer and an official copy of the policy report, to block any information identified by the consumer in the consumer's file as resulting from the alleged identity theft. Additionally, the bill would require the federal banking agencies to jointly establish and maintain guidelines for use in identifying patterns, practices, and specific forms of activity that indicate the possible existence of identity theft.

H.R. 2633, the **Identity Theft Protection and Information Blackout Act of 2003**, includes a number of provisions restricting the sale, purchase, display, and use of an individual's social security number in both the government and private sector. The bill would also deem the refusal to do business without receipt of a social security number an unfair or deceptive act of practice under the Federal Trade Commission

Act, and prohibit the disclosure of a social security number by a consumer reporting agency except in connection with the disclosure of a full consumer credit report furnished in accordance with section 604 of the FCRA. H.R. 2633 also includes provisions aimed at protecting the privacy of medical information in connection with financial transactions, and prohibiting the use of medical information in connection with any decision to offer, provide, or continue to provide any financial product or service.

Chapter 4

FINANCIAL PRIVACY LAWS AFFECTING SHARING OF CUSTOMER INFORMATION AMONG AFFILIATED INSTITUTIONS[*]

M. Maureen Murphy

INTRODUCTION

The privacy provisions of the Gramm-Leach-Bliley Act of 1999 (P.L. 106-102) do not permit customers to preclude financial institutions from sharing nonpublic personal information with affiliated companies; they merely require companies to notify their customers of their practices of information sharing with affiliates. Until the Fair Credit Reporting Act (FCRA) was amended in 1996, sharing of such information with affiliates might have subjected a company to being regulated as a credit reporting agency. Under provisions added in 1996, 15 U.S.C. §§ 1681a(d)(2)(A)(ii) and (iii), which preempt inconsistent state law until January, 1, 2004, companies have been permitted to share among their corporate family a broad range of data they have collected on their customers provided they have given the customers the opportunity to preclude, i.e., opt out of, the information sharing. After January 1, 2004, states may act to override this FCRA provision. While information sharing among affiliates would, thus, not automatically become impermissible on January 1, 2004, the possibility of enactment of state overrides on a piecemeal and inconsistent basis raises concerns among large nationwide conglomerates. This

---

[*] Excerpted from CRS Report RS21427. Updated February 27, 2003.

chapter provides an analysis of the current federal law and a brief description of state laws that appear to provide more consumer protection with respect to the issue of information sharing among affiliates. It will be updated to reflect action on major legislation.

BACKGROUND

Although confidentiality standards for businesses dealing in consumer information have traditionally been a matter of state law, both the Fair Credit Reporting Act of 1970 (FCRA)[1] and the privacy title of the Gramm-Leach-Bliley Act of 1999 (GLBA)[2] have meant that federal law generally controls the dissemination of consumer credit information and governs the disclosing and safeguarding of nonpublic personal information held by a wide array of financial institutions.[3]

GLBA generally prohibits the disclosure of nonpublic personal information on a customer or consumer by financial institutions unless the consumer is given an opportunity to prevent disclosure, i.e., opt-out; but it contains no prohibition on sharing of customer information among affiliates. It requires each financial institution to notify customers of its privacy policies and practices including those related to information sharing with affiliates.[4] FCRA prescribes standards that address information collected by businesses that provide information used to determine eligibility of consumers for credit, insurance, or employment. It imposes requirements for accuracy, limits purposes for which such information may be disseminated, allows certain rights for consumer access, and includes civil and criminal penalties for its violation. It generally defines "consumer reports" and limits the purposes and conditions under which "consumer reports" may be furnished by entities that it refers to and regulates as "consumer reporting agencies."[5]

Apparently, in response to concern that information sharing among affiliated companies might be interpreted as providing consumer reports, thereby subjecting

---

[1] P.L. 91-508, tit. VI, §§ 601 et seq.; 88 *Stat.* 1521;15 U.S.C. §§ 1681 - 1681u.
[2] P.L. 106-102, 113 *Stat.* 1338 (1999).
[3] "Financial institution" is defined to mean "any institution the business of which is engaging in financial activities as defined under section 103 of GLBA, § 4k [12 U.S.C. §1843(k)] of the Bank Holding Company Act of 1956." Essentially, these include banking, securities, and insurance activities as enumerated in GLBA and other activities found by the Board of Governors of the Federal Reserve Board, with the concurrence of the Secretary of the Treasury, either (1) to be financial in nature or (2) not posing a risk to the safety or soundness of depository institutions or the financial system generally and complementary to a financial activity. There are, however, exceptions for persons subject to regulation by the Commodity Futures Trading Commission under the Commodity Exchange Act, entities chartered under the Farm Credit Act of 1971, and entities engaged in secondary market operations as long as they do not transfer nonpublic personal information to a nonaffiliated third party.
[4] 15 U.S.C. § 6803.
[5] 15 U.S.C. § 1681b. See generally, CRS Report RL31666, *Fair Credit Reporting Act:: Rights and Responsibilities.*

banks, insurance companies, and securities firms to all of the obligations imposed upon consumer reporting agencies under the FCRA,[6] the FCRA was amended by the Consumer Credit Reporting Reform Act of 1996.[7] Under these amendments,[8] the FCRA's definition of "consumer report" was amended to exclude communication of transaction and experience information among corporate affiliates and, – provided the consumer was afforded an opportunity to prevent it, i.e., opt out -- communication of other information concerning the consumer among affiliates.[9] Essentially, these provisions permit companies to share with their affiliates certain customer information respecting their transactions and experience with a customer without any notification requirements.[10] Other information about their customers, such as credit reports and application information, may not be shared with other companies in the corporate family unless the customers are given "clear and conspicuous" notice about the sharing and an opportunity to direct that the information not be shared.[11]

FCRA and GLBA Preemption Language

The FCRA preemption of state law regarding affiliate sharing of information is stated in terms of an exception to the rule[12] that the FCRA preempts state law only to the extent of the inconsistency. It reads:

> No requirement or prohibition may be imposed under the laws of any State...(2) with respect to the exchange of information among persons affiliated by common ownership or common corporate control, except that this paragraph shall not apply

---

[6] See, e.g., Joseph L. Seidel, "The Consumer Credit Reporting Reform Act: Information Sharing and Preemption," 2 *North Carolina Banking Institute* 78, 82-83 (1998) (hereinafter, "Seidel"). L. Richard Fischer, Michel F. McEneney, and Clarke D. Camper, "Fair Credit Reporting Act Amendments: Compliance Issues for Banks," 18 *ABA Bank Compliance* 7 (1997) (available in LEXIS, BANKNG Library, ARCNWS file).

[7] P.L. 104-208, Div. A, Tit. II, Subtitle D, Ch. 1, § §2401 2422,2419, 110 *Stat.* 3009, 3009-396 to 3009 - 454.

[8] P.L. 104-208, Div. A, Tit. II, Subtitle D, Ch. 1, § 2419, 110 *Stat.* 3009-452, adding 15 U.S.C.§ 1618t(b)(2).

[9] 15 U.S.C. § 1681a(d)(2)(A).

[10] 15 U.S.C. § 1681a(d)(2)(A)(ii). Notice is required under GLBA, 15 U.S.C. § 6803, which requires disclosure when the customer relationship is formed and annually thereafter of a financial institution's privacy policies and practices, including those relating disclosures to affiliates.

[11] 15 U.S.C. § 1681a(d)(2) (A)(iii).

[12] The FCRA's general preemption clause reads:

> Except as provided in subsections (b) and (c) of this section, this subchapter does not annul, alter, affect, or exempt any person subject to the provisions of this subchapter from complying with the laws of any State with respect to the collection, distribution, or use of any information on consumers, except to the extent that those laws are inconsistent with any provision of this subchapter, and then only to the extent of the inconsistency.
>
> 15 U.S.C. § 1681t(a).

with respect to subsection (a) or (c)(1) of section 2480e of title 9, Vermont Statutes Annotated (as in effect on September 30, 1999)....[13]

After January 1, 2004, states may override the FCRA authorization for interaffiliate sharing of customer information by enacting a provision of state law or of the state's constitution that states explicitly that it is intended to supplement the FCRA provision and that provides greater protection to consumers than the FCRA provision provides.[14] The legislative history of these amendments indicates a Congressional intent to establish a national standard for interaffiliate sharing of information pertinent to the consumer credit industry in the interest of "operational efficiency for industry ... and competitive prices for consumers" in the credit reporting and credit granting [industries that] are, in many aspects, national in scope."[15]

GLBA's prohibitions deal only with sharing of nonpublic personal information by financial institutions with nonaffiliated third parties. There is no direct authorization of sharing such information among affiliated financial institutions. In essence, therefore, GLBA indirectly authorizes interaffiliate sharing of information by a provision disavowing an intent to supercede the FCRA.[16] It, therefore, preserves the conditions placed upon interaffiliate sharing of information in the FCRA: (1) that information other than experience or transaction information may be shared only upon providing customers an opportunity to opt-out; and (2) state laws may not preempt until January 1, 2004, and, then, only upon specified conditions. This preservation of the FCRA runs counter to GLBA's general preemption provision under which GLBA preempts state laws only to the extent that they provide less protection than GLBA.[17] Whether or not a state law provides more protection than GLBA and is not preempted, however, must be determined by the Federal Trade Commission (FTC).[18]

Generally, state laws that provide more protection than GLBA, e.g., that require a specific form of notice respecting an institution's privacy policy, for example, would not automatically be enforceable, without an FTC determination as required under

---

[13] 15 U.S.C. § 1681t(2). The Vermont statute prohibits anyone from obtaining a consumer's credit report without consent or a court order.

[14] 15 U.S.C. § 1681t(d)(2). This specifies that the general exceptions (including that relating to sharing of information among affiliates) to the rule on preemption "do not apply to any provision of State law (including any provision of a State constitution) that–(A) is enacted after January 1, 2004; (B) states explicitly that the provision is intended to supplement this subchapter [15 U.S.C. §§ 1681 - 1671u, i.e., the FCRA]; and (C) gives greater protection to consumers than is provided under this subchapter."

[15] See S. Rep. 104-185, 104th Cong., 1st Sess. (1995), reporting on S. 650 in the 104th Congress, the immediate predecessor of the legislation enacted in 1996. The time limitation derived from a manager's amendment offered by Senator Bryan in an earlier Congress. 140 *Cong. Rec.* S5027 (May 3, 1993 daily ed.).

[16] 15 U.S.C. § 6806.

[17] 15 U.S.C. § 6807.

[18] 15 U.S.C. § 6807(b).

GLBA[19] That would not appear to be true for a state law limiting interaffiliate information sharing, provided that it is enacted after January 1, 2004, and otherwise meets requirements specified in the FCRA.[20] Such state laws would appear to be covered by the GLBA provision specifying that "nothing [subject to unrelated exceptions] in this chapter shall be construed to modify, limit or supersede the operation of the Fair Credit Reporting Act."[21]

Current State Laws and Legislative Activity

Since enactment of GLBA, there has been considerable activity in state legislatures on financial privacy issues, particularly in terms of making reference to the changes wrought by GLBA. Some states have laws that are more protective of consumer privacy. For example, at least four states, Alaska,[22] Connecticut,[23] North Dakota,[24] and Vermont,[25] have current laws that would require an opt-in or in some way hamper the sharing of customer information among affiliates. None of these would, of course, operate to override the FCRA authorization of interaffiliate information sharing without further legislative action. In other states, since GLBA, there have been provisions enacted modifying stringent financial privacy laws to accommodate GLBA.[26] In the only state holding a referendum on such a statute, North Dakota, the voters by a 73% majority, voted to repeal the new law.[27] In the 2003 legislative session, the legislatures of at least two states, California[28] and New

---

[19] 15 U.S.C. § 6807(b).

[20] 15 U.S.C. § 1681t(d)(2). See n. 15 *supra*.

[21] 15 U.S.C. § 6806.

[22] Alaska Stat. § 6.01.028 generally requires customer consent for a financial institution to disclose customer information, with no blanket exception or authorization for sharing information among affiliated companies, although there is permission for sharing with marketing partners.

[23] Connecticut Gen. Stat. Anno. §§ 36a-41 to 36a-44 require consent for disclosure by financial institutions, authorize disclosures in various circumstances, but contain no blanket exception for sharing of information among affiliates and place restrictions on sharing of information with broker-dealers.

[24] N.D. Cent. Code §§ 6.08.1-01 to 6-08.1-08, requires customer written consent for sharing of information among affiliates.

[25] Vermont Stat. Anno. §§ 10201 - 10205 prohibits disclosure of customer financial information by financial institutions except as provided in a list of exceptions, none of which appear to permit interaffiliate sharing of customer information.

[26] See, e.g., Florida Stat. §655.059(2)(b). (Amended to that effect in 2001). This states that "nothing...[in the financial privacy statute] shall prohibit a financial institution from disclosing financial information ...as permitted by [GLBA]."

[27] See Mark Wolski, "North Dakota Voters Trounce Bid to Let Banks Use 'Opt-Out' on Financial Privacy," 78 *BNA's Banking Report* 1051 (June 17, 2002).

[28] California Senate Bill 1, introduced December 2, 2002, would provide a customer opt-out for information sharing among affiliates and an affirmative opt-in for sharing with nonaffiliated third parties. A previous version of the measure had been vetoed by Governor Davis. See Laura Mahoney, "California Senate Kicks off New Session by Bringing Back Financial Privacy Measure," 79 *BNA's Banking Report* 926 (December 9, 2002).

Jersey,[29] are considering enacting laws that would appear to be directed at limiting the ability of financial institutions to share customer information should the FCRA preemption provision not be renewed. Another, New York,[30] is considering legislation to require affirmative consent for disclosing nonpublic personal information to nonaffiliated third parties.

Legislative Issues

The issue of whether or not and under what circumstances to renew the FCRA preemption of state restrictions on affiliate sharing of customer information is likely to be joined with issues relating to other FCRA provisions also subject to the January 1, 2004, expiration date.[31] Consideration of these topics may engender debate on other consumer credit issues–such as preempting state predatory lending laws or state laws restricting insurance companies' use of credit scoring.[32] It may also provoke questions as to whether or not to alter GLBA's privacy provisions. Some of the policy issues that might be considered are: (1) Should GLBA require opt-out for information sharing among affiliates, similar to the FCRA provisions? (2) Should GLBA be modified to require opt-in for sharing with nonaffiliated third parties? (3) Should GLBA be modified to require opt-ins for sharing of sensitive information? (4) If so, how should such sensitive information be defined? and (5) Should the same standards apply to sharing of information among affiliates and to sharing pursuant to joint ventures or marketing agreements–as is the case under GLBA? Underlying these policy issues, of course, are questions that are more general – such as what is to be gained by these privacy laws in terms of effectiveness in preventing unauthorized

---

[29] New Jersey Senate Bill No. 2245, introduced January 16, 2003, would prohibit financial institutions from requiring more information than reasonably necessary and prohibits disclosure of confidential consumer information to affiliates or unaffiliated third parties without obtaining affirmative consent and specifying the types of information that will be disclosed and the conditions under which it will be disclosed. The bill would also provide consumer access to information and opportunity to dispute the accuracy of the information.

[30] New York Assembly Bill 869, introduced January 8, 2003. This legislation would also provide greater protection than GLBA in other ways, such as providing a private right of action.

[31] Without extension of the preemptions, "states could individually determine when a loan would be deemed delinquent, what borrower information a lender could report to credit bureaus, and what fines could be imposed for providing inaccurate information." Rob Blackwell, "Greenspan Is 1st Regulator to Endorse FCRA Extension," *American Banker* 1 (February 13, 2003). (Available in LEXIS, News Library, Curnws file.) Other provisions that are subject to the same conditions for state overrides after January 1, 2004, are provisions relating to: furnishing credit reports in connection with preapproved unsolicited offers of insurance; timing in connection with disputed accuracy of credit reports; certain duties in connection with adverse actions taken on the basis of a credit report; duties in connection with unsolicited, preapproved credit card or insurance offers; certain specifications as to what may and may not be included in consumer reports; and duties of persons furnishing information to credit reporting agencies. 15 U.S.C. § § 1681t(b) and (c).

[32] See ; e.g., "Expiring Info Sharing Pre-Emption May Spark Fight, *National Journal's Congress Daily (January 23, 2003).*

access or dissemination of personal data, deterring identity theft, and meeting justifiable public expectations of privacy.[33] There are also practical matters – such as the relative cost of compliance both to the industry and to its customers. Some of these issues have been addressed in Congressional hearings in the 107th Congress[34] and may resurface in hearings as legislation is developed in the 108th Congress.

---

[33] See CRS Report RS21163 , "Remedies Available to Victims of Identity Theft," and CRS Report RS21803, "Identity Theft and the Fair Credit Reporting Act: An Analysis of *TRW v. Andrews* and Current Legislation."

[34] See, U.S. Senate Comm. on Banking, Housing, and Urban Affairs, "Hearing on 'Financial Privacy and Consumer Protection," [http://banking.senate.gov/hrg02.htm#sep02]; The House Committee on Energy and Commerce held hearings covering a wide variety of topics. [http://energycommerce.house.gov/107/action/action.htm]. Included are: EU Data Protection Directive; privacy in the commercial world, and existing federal statutes addressing information privacy.

Chapter 5

AWARENESS AND USE OF EXISTING DATA ON IDENTITY THEFT[‡]

Richard M. Stana

This chapter reviews federal and state efforts to address identity theft, which has been characterized by law enforcement as the fastest growing type of crime in the United States. As noted in our May 1998 report,[1] identity theft or identity fraud generally involves "stealing" another person's personal identifying information—such as Social Security number (SSN), date of birth, and mother's maiden name—and then using the information to fraudulently establish credit, run up debt, or take over existing financial accounts. Later that year, Congress passed the Identity Theft and Assumption Deterrence Act of 1998 (the Identity Theft Act).[2] Enacted in October 1998, the federal statute made identity theft a separate crime against the person whose identity was stolen, broadened the scope of the offense to include the misuse of information as well as documents, and provided punishment—generally a fine or imprisonment for up to 15 years or both. Also, since 1998, most states have enacted laws that criminalize identity theft. Thus, various federal and numerous state and local law enforcement agencies are responsible for investigating identity theft crimes. Relevant federal agencies include the Secret Service, the Federal Bureau of Investigation (FBI), and the Postal Inspection Service, as well as the Social Security

---

[‡] Excerptedf from General Accounting Office (GAO) Report GAO-02-766.
[1] U.S. General Accounting Office, *Identity Fraud: Information on Prevalence, Cost, and Internet Impact is Limited*, GAO/GGD-98-100BR (Washington, D.C.: May 1, 1998) and *Identity Fraud: Prevalence and Cost Appear to be Growing*, GAO-02-363 (Washington, D.C.: Mar. 1, 2002).
[2] Public Law 105-318 (1998).

Administration's (SSA) Office of the Inspector General (OIG), which receives SSN misuse and other identity theft-related allegations on its fraud hotline.

The passage of federal and state identity theft legislation indicates that this type of crime has been widely recognized as a serious problem across the nation. Now, a current focus for policymakers and criminal justice administrators is to ensure that these laws are effectively enforced.

Specifically, this chapter provides information on

- law enforcement results (such as examples of prosecutions and convictions) under the federal Identity Theft Act;
- law enforcement results under state statutes that, similar to the federal act, provide state and local law enforcement officials with the tools to prosecute and convict identity theft criminals;
- the means used to promote cooperation or coordination among federal, state, and local law enforcement agencies in addressing identity theft crimes that span multiple jurisdictions; and
- actions taken by the SSA/OIG to resolve SSN misuse and other identity theft-related allegations received during fiscal year 1999.

To address these questions, we interviewed responsible officials and reviewed documentation obtained from the Department of Justice and its components, including the Executive Office for United States Attorneys (EOUSA) and the FBI; the Department of the Treasury and its components, including the Secret Service and the Internal Revenue Service (IRS); the SSA/OIG; and the Federal Trade Commission (FTC). Also, we conducted a literature search to obtain examples of cases prosecuted under the federal Identity Theft Act. Regarding state and local law enforcement efforts, we focused on 10 states—Arizona, California, Florida, Georgia, Illinois, Michigan, New Jersey, Pennsylvania, Texas, and Wisconsin—which we judgmentally selected on the basis of having either the highest incidences of reported identity theft or the longest-standing applicable statutes. We conducted our work from July 2001 to May 2002 in accordance with generally accepted auditing standards.

RESULTS IN BRIEF

We found no comprehensive or centralized data on enforcement results under the federal Identity Theft Act. However, according to a Deputy Assistant Attorney General, federal prosecutors are using the 1998 federal law. Moreover, in response to our inquiries, Justice Department Criminal Division officials said that federal prosecutors consider the Identity Theft Act to be a useful statute because it provides broad jurisdiction and is another tool to use in combating white-collar or financial crimes—such as bank fraud, credit card fraud, and mail fraud—that typically have elements of identity theft. Our review of selected cases prosecuted under the federal act illustrate that identity theft generally is not a stand-alone crime. Rather, identity theft typically is a component of one or more other white-collar or financial crimes.

As with the federal act, we found no centralized or comprehensive data on enforcement results under state identity theft statutes. However, officials in the 10 states we selected for study provided us with examples of actual investigations or prosecutions under these statutes. Presented for illustration purposes only, these cases are not necessarily representative of identity theft crimes in these or other states. Officials we contacted in these states also noted various continuing challenges encountered in enforcing identity theft statutes. For instance, because identity theft is still a "nontraditional" crime, some police departments may be unaware of the importance of taking reports of identity theft, much less initiating investigations. Also, it is important that law enforcement resources be allocated to meet priorities. In this regard, officials in several of the 10 states told us that limited resources are allocated to priorities such as violent crimes and drug offenses and, thus, the number of investigators and prosecutors for addressing identity theft often is insufficient. Further, according to some of the officials we contacted, because many identity theft cases present multi- or cross-jurisdictional issues—such as when a perpetrator steals personal information in one city and uses the information to conduct fraudulent activities in another city or state—law enforcement agencies sometimes tend to view identity theft as being "someone else's problem."

Generally, the prevalence of identity theft and the frequently multi- or cross-jurisdictional nature of such crime underscore the importance of having means for promoting cooperation or coordination among federal, state, and local law enforcement agencies. One of the most commonly used means of coordination, task forces, can have participating agencies from all levels of law enforcement—federal, state, and local—and, in some instances, can have participants from banks and other private sector entities. Another relevant coordination entity is the U.S. Attorney General's Identity Theft Subcommittee, whose membership includes various federal law enforcement and regulatory agencies, as well as state and local representation. In 1999, among other purposes, the Attorney General's White Collar Crime Council established the subcommittee to promote cooperation and coordination in addressing identity theft cases involving multiple jurisdictions.

Another vehicle for coordination is the FTC's Consumer Sentinel Network, which is a secure, encrypted Web site for use by law enforcement agencies. In 1999, FTC established a central database (the Identity Theft Data Clearinghouse) to collect information reported by identity theft victims. Law enforcement agencies can use the Consumer Sentinel Network to access the Clearinghouse database and scan consumer complaints matching certain criteria to determine, for example, if there is a larger pattern of criminal activity. However, relatively few law enforcement agencies have used the Consumer Sentinel Network, and centralized analysis of database information to generate investigative leads and referrals has also been limited. FTC staff said that the availability of the database as an aid for law enforcement is still relatively new and some potential users may still be unaware of this investigative resource. We are recommending that the Attorney General have the Identity Theft Subcommittee promote greater awareness and use of the Consumer Sentinel Network and the Clearinghouse database by all levels of law enforcement.

While SSA/OIG's fraud hotline annually receives thousands of allegations involving either (1) SSN misuse or (2) program fraud with SSN misuse potential, the agency concentrates its investigative resources on the latter category of allegations because the protection of Social Security trust funds is a priority. In these 2 categories, SSA/OIG received approximately 62,000 allegations in fiscal year 1999, and the agency opened investigative cases on 4,636 (about 7 percent) of these allegations. About three in four of the investigative cases involved program fraud-related allegations. SSA/OIG statistics for investigative cases opened in fiscal year 1999 indicate that a total of 1,347 cases had resulted in criminal convictions or other judicial actions, as of April 30, 2002. During our review, the SSA Inspector General told us that his office does not have enough investigators to address all of the SSN misuse allegations received on the agency's fraud hotline. However, FTC staff noted that, starting in February 2001, FTC began to routinely upload information from SSA/OIG's fraud hotline about these allegations into FTC's Identity Theft Data Clearinghouse, thereby making the information available to law enforcement agencies via the Consumer Sentinel Network.

In a letter dated June 19, 2002, the Department of Justice generally agreed with the substance of this chapter and the recommendation made. Further, Justice noted several actions that it has taken or will take to directly address the recommendation.

BACKGROUND

Under the federal Identity Theft Act, a criminal offense is committed if a person "knowingly transfers or uses, without lawful authority, a means of identification of another person with the intent to commit, or to aid or abet, any unlawful activity that constitutes a violation of Federal law, or that constitutes a felony under any applicable State or local law ..." The relevant section of this legislation is codified at 18 U.S.C. § 1028(a)(7)("fraud and related activity in connection with identification documents and information"). According to an analysis of the new law by the United States Sentencing Commission:[3]

- Before passage of the 1998 act, the unauthorized use or transfer of identity documents was illegal under title 18 of the U.S. Code, section 1028—which included subsections (a)(1) through (a)(6). The unauthorized use of credit cards, personal identification numbers, automated teller machine codes, and other electronic access devices was illegal under another section of the U.S. Code—that is, 18 U.S.C. § 1029 ("fraud and related activity in connection with access devices").

- The addition of subsection (a)(7) to section 1028 expanded the definition of "means of identification" to include such information as SSN and other government identification numbers, dates of birth, and unique biometric data (e.g., fingerprints), as well as electronic access devices and routing codes used in the financial and telecommunications sectors.

- Under the Identity Theft Act, the new definition of means of identification includes prior statutory definitions of "identification documents."

According to the United States Sentencing Commission, a key impact is to make the proscriptions of the new identity theft law applicable to a wide range of offense conduct, which can be independently prosecuted under numerous existing statutes. That is, any unauthorized use of means of identification can now be charged either as a violation of the new law or in conjunction with other federal statutes.

In further elaboration of the breadth of the definition of means of identification and its impact, the Sentencing Commission's analysis noted the following:

- The new law covers offense conduct already covered by a multitude of other federal statutes. The unauthorized use of credit cards, for instance, is already prosecuted under 18 U.S.C. § 1029, but now also can be prosecuted under the newly enacted 18 U.S.C. § 1028(a)(7).

- Other examples of offense conduct include providing a false SSN or other identification number to obtain a tax refund and presenting false passports or immigration documents by using the names and addresses and photos of lawful residents or citizens to enter the United States.

---

[3] United States Sentencing Commission, Economic Crimes Policy Team, *Identity Theft Final Report* (Washington, D.C.: Dec. 15, 1999).

In total, according to the Sentencing Commission, the violation of some 180 federal criminal statutes can potentially fall within the ambit of 18 U.S.C. § 1028(a)(7).

Regarding state statutes, at the time of our 1998 report, only a few states had specific laws to address identity theft. Now, as table 1 shows, 44 states have specific laws that address identity theft, and 5 other states have laws that cover activities included within the definition of identity theft. Almost one-half (22) of these 49 states enacted relevant laws in 1999. According to FTC's analysis, identity theft can be a felony offense in 45 of the 49 states that have laws to address this crime.[4]

Table 1: States That Have Identity Theft Statutes
(by Year of Enactment)

Year of enactment	States with specific laws to address identity theft	Number
1996	Arizona	1
1997	California and Wisconsin	2
1998	Georgia, Kansas, Massachusetts, Mississippi,[a] and West Virginia	5
1999	Arkansas, Connecticut, Florida, Idaho, Illinois, Iowa, Louisiana, Maryland, Minnesota, Missouri, Nevada, New Hampshire, New Jersey, North Carolina, North Dakota, Ohio, Oklahoma, Oregon, Tennessee, Texas, Washington, and Wyoming	22
2000	Delaware, Kentucky, Michigan, Pennsylvania, Rhode Island, South Carolina, South Dakota, Utah, and Virginia	9
2001	Alabama, Alaska, Indiana, Montana, and New Mexico	5
Total		44

Note: According to the FTC, five other states—Colorado, Hawaii, Nebraska, New York, and Maine—have laws that cover activities included within the definition of identity theft but are not coterminous with it, and one other state (Vermont) is collecting data to consider enacting possible identity theft legislation.

[a] Mississippi possibly enacted the nation's first identity theft statute (Miss. Code Ann. § 97-19-85), even though it was titled as a "false pretenses" statute rather than specifically labeled as an "identity theft" statute. Originally enacted in 1993, the statute was amended in 1998 to include additional identifiers and increase punishment from a misdemeanor to a felony.

Source: FTC data. Also, note "a" is based on our analysis of the Mississippi statute and a follow-up discussion with an official in the Mississippi Attorney General's Office.

In the view of Justice Department Criminal Division officials, the enactment of state identity theft laws has multi-jurisdictional benefits to all levels of law enforcement—federal, state, and local. In explanation, Justice officials commented that the various state statutes, coupled with the federal statute, provide a broader

---

[4] Many state statutes provide that identity theft of credit, money, goods, services, or other property over certain amounts is a felony. Under the specified amounts, the offense would be a criminal misdemeanor.

framework for addressing identity theft, particularly when a multi-agency task force approach is used. The Justice officials noted, for instance, that it is very plausible for a task force to generate multiple cases, some of which can result in federal prosecutions and others in state or local prosecutions.

Generally, law enforcement agencies widely acknowledge that SSNs often are used as identifiers by thieves to obtain or "breed" other identification documentation. Through its fraud hotline, SSA/OIG annually receives thousands of allegations of fraud, waste, and abuse. Most of these allegations are classified by SSA/OIG as involving either (1) SSN misuse or (2) program fraud that may contain elements of SSN misuse. In these two categories, SSA/OIG received about 62,000 allegations in fiscal year 1999, about 83,000 allegations in fiscal year 2000, and about 104,000 allegations in fiscal year 2001. SSA/OIG officials explained these two categories of allegations as follows:

- Allegations of "SSN misuse" include, for example, incidents where a criminal uses the SSN of another individual for the purpose of fraudulently obtaining credit, establishing utility services, or acquiring goods. SSNs are also misused to violate immigration laws, flee the criminal justice system by assuming a new identity, or obtain personal information to stalk an individual. Generally, this category of allegations does not directly involve SSA program benefits.

- On the other hand, allegations of fraud in SSA programs for the aged, survivors, or disabled often entail some element of SSN misuse. For example, a criminal may use the victim's SSN or other identifying information for the purpose of obtaining Social Security benefits. When hotline staff receive this type of allegation, it is to be classified under the appropriate category of program fraud.

In 1999, SSA/OIG analyzed a sample of SSN misuse allegations and determined that about 82 percent of such allegations related directly to identity theft.[5] The analysis covered a statistical sample of 400 allegations from a universe of 16,375 allegations received by the fraud hotline from October 1997 through March 1999. The analysis did not cover the other category mentioned previously, that is, allegations of program-related fraud with SSN misuse potential.

---

[5] SSA/OIG, *Management Advisory Report – Analysis of Social Security Number Misuse Allegations Made to the Social Security Administration's Fraud Hotline* (A-15-99-92019, Aug. 1999).

NO COMPREHENSIVE DATA ON LAW ENFORCEMENT RESULTS UNDER THE FEDERAL IDENTITY THEFT ACT, BUT CASE EXAMPLES ILLUSTRATE USE OF THE LAW

There are no comprehensive statistics on the number of investigations, convictions, or other law enforcement results under the Identity Theft Act. As noted in our March 2002 report,[6] federal law enforcement agencies generally do not have information systems that facilitate specific tracking of identity theft cases. For example, while the amendments made by the Identity Theft Act are included as subsection (a)(7) of section 1028, Title 18 of the U.S. Code, EOUSA does not have comprehensive statistics on offenses charged specifically under that subsection. EOUSA officials explained that, except for certain firearms statutes, staff are required to record cases only to the U.S. Code section, not the subsection or the sub-subsection.

Given the absence of comprehensive statistics, we obtained relevant anecdotes or examples of actual investigations and prosecutions under the federal statute. For instance, about 2 years after passage of the Identity Theft Act, a senior Department of Justice official testified at a May 2001 congressional hearing that U.S. Attorneys' Offices throughout the nation were making substantial use of the new federal law that recognized identity theft as a separate crime.[7] In testimony, the Justice official said that federal prosecutors had used the new statute—18 U.S.C. § 1028(a)(7)—in at least 92 cases to date. One example cited in the testimony involved a defendant who stole private bank account information about an insurance company's policyholders and used that information to withdraw funds from the accounts of the policyholders and deposit approximately 4,300 counterfeit bank drafts totaling more than $764,000. The case was prosecuted in the Central District of California. The defendant pled guilty to identity theft and related charges and was sentenced to 27 months of imprisonment and 5 years of supervised release.

Another case cited by the Justice official illustrates that identity theft crimes can have fact-pattern elements encompassing more than one jurisdiction. The case involved a California resident, who committed fraudulent acts in the state of Washington by, among other means, using a Massachusetts driver's license bearing the name of an actual person not associated with the criminal activities. Also, this case further illustrates that identity theft is rarely a stand-alone crime; rather, it frequently is a component of one or more white-collar or financial crimes, such as bank fraud,

---

[6] GAO-02-363.
[7] Prepared statement of Mr. Bruce Swartz, Deputy Assistant Attorney General, Criminal Division, U.S. Department of Justice, for a hearing ("On-line Fraud and Crime: Are Consumers Safe?") before the Subcommittee on Commerce, Trade, and Consumer Protection, House Committee on Energy and Commerce (May 23, 2001).

credit card or access device fraud, or wire fraud. Pertinent details of this case, prosecuted in the Western District of Washington, are as follows:

- Over a period of time in 1999 and 2000, the defendant and other conspirators assumed the identities of third persons without their consent and authorization and fraudulently used the SSNs and names of actual persons. Also, the conspirators created false identity documents, such as state identification cards, driver's licenses, and immigration cards. Using the identities and names of third persons, the conspirators opened banking and investment accounts at numerous locations and obtained credit cards.

- The defendant and other conspirators presented and deposited at least 12 counterfeit checks (valued in excess of $1 million) to various banks and investment companies in western Washington. Also, the conspirators purchased legitimate cashiers checks, in nominal amounts, and then altered them to reflect substantially greater amounts. The conspirators presented or deposited at least five altered checks (worth almost $350,000) in the Seattle area.

According to Justice, in July 2000, the defendant pled guilty to committing three felony counts of identity theft, conspiring to commit wire fraud involving attempted losses in excess of $1 million, and using an unauthorized credit card.

During our current review, Justice Department Criminal Division officials told us that federal prosecutors consider the Identity Theft Act to be a very useful statute. The officials said, for instance, that prosecutors endorse the statute because it provides broad jurisdiction. Further, the Justice officials noted that the Identity Theft Act provides another tool for prosecutors to use, even though in many instances the defendants may be charged under other white-collar crime statutes. The officials explained that identity theft is rarely a stand-alone crime. Thus, cases involving identity theft or identity fraud may have charges under a variety of different statutes relating to these defendants' other crimes, such as bank fraud, credit card fraud, or mail fraud.

No Comprehensive Data on Enforcement Results under State Identity Theft Statutes, but Case Examples Illustrate Use of Such Laws

As with the federal Identity Theft Act, we found no centralized or comprehensive data on enforcement results under state identity theft statutes. However, officials in selected states provided us with examples of actual cases illustrating the use of such statutes. Also, officials in these states noted various challenges encountered in enforcing identity theft statutes—challenges involving topics such as the filing of police reports, the use of limited resources, and the resolution of jurisdictional issues.

Case Examples Illustrate Use of State Identity Theft Laws

The crime of identity theft is not specifically recorded as an offense category in the FBI's Uniform Crime Reporting (UCR) Program.[8] Further, our inquiries with various national organizations—the National Association of Attorneys General, the National District Attorneys Association, and the International Association of Chiefs of Police—indicated that these entities do not have comprehensive data on arrests or convictions under state identity theft laws.

In the absence of national data on enforcement of state identity theft laws, we contacted officials in 10 states—Arizona, California, Florida, Georgia, Illinois, Michigan, New Jersey, Pennsylvania, Texas, and Wisconsin.[9] As table 2 shows, each of these 10 states has a specific statute that makes identity theft a crime and provides for imprisonment of convicted offenders. The length of imprisonment varies by state, ranging upward to as long as 30 years.

---

[8] The UCR Program is a nationwide, cooperative statistical effort of nearly 17,000 city, county, and state law enforcement agencies voluntarily reporting data on crimes brought to their attention. According to the FBI, during 2000, law enforcement agencies active in the UCR Program represented nearly 254 million U.S. inhabitants, or 94 percent of the total population as established by the Bureau of the Census.

[9] We judgmentally selected these states on the basis of their having either the highest incidences of reported identity theft or the longest-standing applicable statutes (see app. I).

Table 2: Sentencing Provisions of Selected States' Identity Theft Laws

State	State code citation	Sentencing provisions
Arizona	Ariz. Rev. Stat. § 13-2008	Imprisonment of 2-1/2 to 12 years.
California	Cal. Penal Code § 530.5	Imprisonment not to exceed 1 year, or fines up to $10,000, or both.
Florida	Fla. Stat. Ann. § 817.568	Imprisonment of up to 5 years and fines up to $5,000, or both. In addition, the defendant may be ordered to pay up to double the pecuniary gain of the defendant or pecuniary loss of the victim.
Georgia	Ga. Code Ann. §§ 16-9-121	Imprisonment of 1 to 10 years and the defendant may be ordered to make restitution.
Illinois	720 Ill. Comp. Stat. 5/16G	Imprisonment from 1 to 30 years.
Michigan	Mich. Comp. Laws § 750.285	Imprisonment up to 5 years, or fines up to $10,000, or both.
New Jersey	N.J. Stat. Ann. § 2C: 21-17	Imprisonment up to 10 years.
Pennsylvania	18 Pa. Cons. Stat. Ann. § 4120	Imprisonment up to 10 years, or fines up to $25,000, or both
Texas	Tex. Penal Code § 32.51	Imprisonment up to 10 years and a fine not to exceed $10,000.
Wisconsin	Wis. Stat. § 943.201	Imprisonment up to 10 years, or fines up to $10,000, or both

Source: GAO summary of state statutes.

As with the national organizations we contacted, state officials could not provide aggregate data on law enforcement results (e.g., total number of arrests, prosecutions, or convictions) under their respective state's identity theft statute. However, the officials were able to provide us with examples of actual cases prosecuted under these statutes. The following sections discuss case examples for three states—California, Michigan, and Texas. Presented for illustration purposes only, these cases are not necessarily representative of identity theft crimes in these or other states. Also, as with federal cases, the state case examples also indicate that identity theft can be a component of other crimes, such as check and credit card fraud, as well as computer-related crimes.

California: High Prevalence of Identity Theft

Effective January 1, 1998, under section 530.5 of the California Penal Code, any person "who willfully obtains personal information ... of another person without the authorization of that person, and uses that information for any unlawful purpose, including to obtain, or attempt to obtain credit, goods, services, or medical information in the name of the person without the consent of that person, is guilty of a public offense."[10] According to the officials we contacted in California, there is not a centralized source of aggregate or statewide statistics regarding the number of investigations, arrests, or prosecutions under California's identity theft statute. However, federal law enforcement officials told us that, relative to many other states, the prevalence of identity theft appears to be high in California. The federal officials also commented that new or different types of identity theft schemes often appear to originate on the west coast and then spread east.

Regarding identity theft cases handled at the state level, in October 2001, one California deputy attorney general told us that she was handling four active cases, and she commented that these were a "tiny drop in the bucket" in reference to prevalence. Further, she noted that the four active cases had one thing in common, that is, the number of victims was "in the hundreds" or even "never ending." Also, in October 2001, another California deputy attorney general told us that, at an identity theft conference hosted by the California attorney general in May 2001, two local law enforcement agencies reported thousands of active cases. Specifically, the Los Angeles County Sheriff's Office reported 2,000 active cases, and the Los Angeles Police Department reported 5,000 active cases.

More recently, in March 2002, we contacted the Los Angeles Police Department to obtain updated information. According to the detective supervisor of the Identity Theft and Credit Card Squad, over 8,000 cases of identity theft were reported to the department in calendar year 2001. He estimated that about 70 percent of these identity theft-related cases involved utility or cellular telephone fraud and the other 30 percent involved credit card fraud and check fraud. Further, the detective supervisor said that the department accepts reports of identity theft only if the victim is a resident of Los Angeles.

Michigan: Cases under the State's 5-year Felony Statute

Michigan's identity theft statute—codified at Mich. Comp. Laws § 750.285—was adopted by the state legislature on December 7, 2000, and became effective April 1, 2001. This new law created a 5-year felony offense for identity theft, making it illegal for a person to obtain or attempt to obtain, without authorization, the "personal identity information" of another person with the intent to use that information unlawfully to (1) obtain financial credit, employment, or access to medical records or information contained in them; (2) purchase or otherwise obtain or lease any real or personal property; or (3) commit any illegal act. One state-level entity that handles investigations and prosecutions of identity theft is the High Tech Crime Unit of the Michigan Department of the Attorney General. This unit deals with computer crimes

---

[10] According to a California deputy attorney general, the state's identity theft statute was amended in 2000 to remove certain language (i.e., "without the authorization") in order to cover cases where victims give information willingly (e.g., to car rental companies), but the information is later used for unlawful purposes.

and crimes committed over the Internet—crimes in which identity theft is often an aspect.

According to the Michigan assistant attorney general who serves as Chief of the High Tech Crime Unit, the state's first criminal prosecution under the 5-year felony statute was initiated by the unit in August 2001. In this case, a woman was charged with stealing personal identity information from her former employer, using that information to apply over the Internet for several credit cards, and making purchases (approximately $1,000) on such cards, without authorization. The woman pled guilty and was sentenced to 1 year probation and required to pay restitution. The Chief also said that, as of June 2002, three other cases were pending under Michigan's identity theft statute.

We also contacted the Office of the Prosecuting Attorney for Oakland County, Michigan.[11] A deputy prosecutor told us that in the approximately 8 months since Michigan's identity theft statute has been in effect—that is, from April 1, 2001, to the time of our inquiry in early December 2001—one case had been initiated in Oakland County under the statute. This official said that the case, which involved a defendant who had obtained the victim's personal information and used it to apply for a credit card, was still ongoing in the county's court system.

Texas: State Statute Modeled after Federal Law

Texas' identity theft statute—codified at Texas Penal Code § 32.51—became effective September 1, 1999. Modeled after the federal Identity Theft Act, a person commits the offense of identity theft under Texas' law if he or she "obtains, possesses, transfers, or uses identifying information of another person without the other person's consent or with intent to harm or defraud another." According to officials we contacted in Texas, there is not a centralized source of aggregate or statewide statistics regarding the number of identity theft investigations, arrests, or prosecutions under Texas Penal Code § 32.51

In response to our inquiry, the Internet Bureau of the Texas Attorney General's Office reported that it had opened 12 identity theft cases during the period September 2000 through August 2001. According to an Internet Bureau official, these cases had resulted in three arrests and indictments, as of November 2001. In one of these cases, a temporary employee of a technology company allegedly stole personal identifying information from the company's employee database and provided the information to an accomplice, who used the information to apply for bank credit online and collect fees paid by the banks for each application. Reportedly, the scheme affected hundreds of employees. The Internet Bureau official told us that each application using a stolen

---

[11] The Oakland County Prosecuting Attorney's Office is located in Pontiac, Michigan. According to a deputy prosecutor, investigations of crimes are handled by each of the 42 local police departments in the county.

identity was considered a separate violation and that two suspects had been criminally charged.

We also contacted the Dallas County District Attorney's Office. While the office did not have any readily available statistics on identity theft cases, an assistant district attorney said that the office had handled a variety of identity theft cases, involving check and credit card fraud, as well as fraudulent purchases of vehicles and the acquisition of utility services. The assistant district attorney noted that some of these crimes had been perpetrated by organized rings. One example cited involved a group of three individuals, who made approximately $750,000 in illegal transactions in less than 180 days by using identity fraud coupled with other traditional crimes such as credit card abuse, forgery of commercial instruments, and securing loans through deception.

Enforcement Challenges Regarding State Statutes

Generally, many of the 10 states' officials with whom we talked noted various challenges or obstacles to enforcing identity theft statutes. As discussed in the following sections, these challenges involved topics such as the filing of police reports, the use of limited resources, and the resolution of jurisdictional issues.

Local Police Are Not Always Documenting Identity Theft Crimes Reported by Victims

Efforts taken by identity theft victims to file reports with law enforcement agencies are an important first step in being able to investigate such crime. Also, police reports can be useful to consumers who are victims of identity theft and who need to provide documentation of such to creditors and debt collectors. However, FTC data show that 59 percent of the victims who contacted the FTC during a 12-month period (Nov. 1999 through Oct. 2000) had already contacted the police, but 35 percent of these victims reported that they could not get a police report. Partly because identity theft is still a non-traditional crime, some police departments are unaware of the importance of taking reports of identity theft, much less initiating investigations.

To help address this issue, FTC staff, in conjunction with the Identity Theft Subcommittee, began working with the International Association of Chiefs of Police to encourage police officers to write police reports for victims of identity theft. As a result, in November 2000, the association adopted a resolution calling for "all law enforcement agencies in the United States to take more positive actions in recording all incidents of identity theft." Regarding the need for more positive actions, the resolution noted thats

"... reports of identity theft to local law enforcement agencies are often handled with the response 'please contact your credit card company,' and often no official report is created or maintained, causing great difficulty in accounting for and tracing these crimes, and leaving the public with the impression their local police department does not care..."

According to FTC staff, even though the association's resolution is not binding, it sends an important message to police around the country. Also, FTC staff indicated that the same message has been reinforced by FTC staff in numerous law enforcement conferences throughout the nation. FTC data show that 46 percent of the victims who contacted the FTC in calendar year 2001 reported that they had already contacted a police department, and 18 percent of these victims reported that they could not get a police report—which represents a reduction of about half from the percentage of victims who reported being unable to get a police report in the November 1999 through October 2000 period.

Despite progress, the importance of police reports is a topic for continuing focus. For example, in January 2002, a Florida study reported that some of the state's law enforcement agencies "are reluctant to take identity theft complaints and do not generate reports in some cases."[12] Consequently, the study recommended that "all law enforcement agencies be required to generate a report on identity theft complaints regardless of their subsequent decision on whether or not they will investigate the case."

Also, during our review, a federal official told us that a continuing priority of the Attorney General's Identity Theft Subcommittee[13] is to help educate local police departments about the critical first step of taking reports from victims of identity theft crime. In this regard, the Secret Service is developing a police training video with the cooperation of the FTC, Department of Justice, and the International Association of Chiefs of Police, which is anticipated to be completed by September 30, 2002. Among other purposes, the training video is to emphasize the importance of police reports in identity theft cases.

State Officials Cited Insufficient Resources as an Obstacle to More Fully Addressing Identity Theft

Officials in several of the 10 states included in our study told us that the level of resources being allocated to investigate and prosecute identity theft often is

---

[12] First interim report of the Sixteenth Statewide Grand Jury, *Statewide Grand Jury Report – Identity Theft in Florida*, in the Supreme Court of the State of Florida (Case No. SC 01-1095, Jan. 10, 2002). Members of the Sixteenth Statewide Grand Jury were empaneled by the Florida Supreme Court at the request of the state's governor to investigate and address identity theft-related issues as they occur in Florida.

[13] As discussed in more detail later in this report, the subcommittee was established in 1999 to foster coordination of investigative and prosecutorial strategies and promote consumer education programs.

insufficient. This observation was voiced, for example, by a deputy district attorney in California (Los Angeles County), who told us that there are not enough investigators and prosecutors to handle the county's identity theft cases.

Similar comments were provided to us by a supervisor in the Consumer Fraud Division of the Illinois Cook County State's Attorney's Office, which reportedly is the second largest prosecutor's office in the nation, with over 900 assistant state's attorneys. In addition to noting that more prosecutors and support staff were needed to effectively combat identity theft, the supervisor commented that funds were needed for training local police agencies how to handle the more complex cases involving multiple victims, multiple jurisdictions, and voluminous documents.

Further, a chief deputy attorney in the Philadelphia District Attorney's Office commented that, given competing priorities and other factors, there is little incentive for police departments in Pennsylvania to allocate resources for investigating identity theft cases. This official said that police departments are more inclined to use their limited resources for investigating violent crimes and drug offenses rather than handling complicated identity theft cases that, even if successfully prosecuted, often lead to relatively light sentences. In explanation, the chief deputy attorney noted the following:

- Identity theft cases require highly trained investigators, require longer-than-usual efforts, and often end without an arrest.

- Also, under the state's identity theft statute, the first offense is a misdemeanor, although identity theft may be a "lesser included offense" with felony charges involving forgery and theft, given that the fact patterns of these crimes may overlap.

- Even when convictions are obtained, identity theft cases generally do not result in long sentences. For instance, to get a minimum prison term of 1 year for an economic crime in Pennsylvania, a defendant probably would have to steal approximately $100,000. In contrast, a felony drug case conviction involving more than 2 grams of cocaine or heroin—an amount with a street value of about $200—has a mandatory minimum sentence of 1 year of imprisonment.

Despite resource and other challenges, the chief deputy attorney said that the Philadelphia District Attorney's Office does handle identity theft cases. He estimated, for instance, that the office investigated about 100 to 200 identity theft cases in calendar year 2000, and he said these cases represented a "small fraction" of the total number of reported cases in Philadelphia.

State Officials Cited Jurisdiction Issues as an Obstacle to More Fully Addressing Identity Theft

According to many of the state and local officials we contacted, jurisdiction and venue problems are common in identity theft cases. The officials noted, for instance, that many identity theft cases present cross-jurisdictional issues, such as when a perpetrator steals personal information in one city and uses the information to conduct fraudulent activities in another city or another state. In this regard, an official in one state told us that law enforcement agencies sometimes tend to view identity theft as being "someone else's problem." That is, the police department in the victim's area of residence refer the victim to the police department in another county or state where the perpetrator used the personal information—and, in turn, the remote police department refers the victim back to the area-of-residence police department.

To help mitigate this type of problem, some of the states' identity theft statutes have provisions that permit multiple counties to have jurisdiction. For example, Arizona's identity theft statute has a provision that allows victims to file reports in any jurisdiction within the state where the theft or related activities arising from the theft occur. Thus, if a credit card is stolen in Phoenix and used in Tempe, the victim may file in either jurisdiction. Similarly, Florida modified its identity theft statute, effective July 1, 2001, to specify that the crime of identity theft can be investigated and prosecuted in the county in which the victim resides or where any element of the crime occurred. Also, during our study, a Wisconsin Department of Justice official told us that consideration was being given to amending Wisconsin's identity theft law to permit prosecution of such crime in the jurisdiction of the victim's residence, in addition to any jurisdiction where the stolen personal identity information was fraudulently used.

FEDERAL, STATE, AND LOCAL LAW ENFORCEMENT AGENCIES USE VARIOUS MEANS TO PROMOTE COOPERATION OR COORDINATION IN ADDRESSING IDENTITY THEFT CRIMES

Many federal, state, and local law enforcement agencies have roles in investigating and prosecuting identity theft. Federal agencies include, for example, the FBI, Secret Service, IRS (Criminal Investigation), Postal Inspection Service, and SSA/OIG, as well as U.S. Attorney Offices. However, most identity theft crimes fall within the responsibility of local investigators and prosecutors—such as city police departments or county sheriffs' offices and county district attorney offices, although state-level agencies, such as state attorney general offices, also have a role.

Generally, the prevalence of identity theft and the frequently multi- or cross-jurisdictional nature of such crime underscore the importance of having means for promoting cooperation or coordination among federal, state, and local law enforcement agencies. One such means is the establishment of law enforcement task forces with multi-agency participation. Other relevant means include a coordinating entity (the Attorney General's Identity Theft Subcommittee) and an information-sharing database (accessible via the FTC's Consumer Sentinel Network) established with federal leadership. However, as discussed in the following sections, there are opportunities for promoting greater awareness and use of the Consumer Sentinel Network.

Law Enforcement Task Forces that Address Identity Theft

The use of task forces is perhaps the most commonly used means for promoting cooperation or coordination among law enforcement agencies to address identity theft cases involving multiple jurisdictions. A main advantage of task forces, according to Secret Service officials, is that the pooling of resources and expertise results in more thorough investigations and better continuity from inception of the investigations through prosecution. The officials also noted that improved interagency relationships result in the sharing of investigative leads, bridging of jurisdictional boundaries, and avoiding duplication of efforts. Regarding the views of state officials, a California deputy attorney general, who was working on a task force that included federal and local law enforcement agencies, told us that this approach simplified all aspects of multi-jurisdictional issues, particularly given that each agency has its own "go to" person.

Generally, task forces can have participating agencies from all levels of law enforcement—federal, state, and local—and may also have private sector representation. The following sections provide examples of task forces developed by federal (Secret Service) and state (California and Florida) leadership, respectively. The scope of our work did not include assessing the effectiveness of these task forces.

Secret Service Task Force Efforts

At the time of our review, the Secret Service was the lead agency in 38 task forces across the country that were primarily targeting financial and electronic crimes—categories of crimes that frequently have identity theft-related elements.[14]

---

[14] Of the 38 task forces, the Secret Service categorized 24 as being financial crimes task forces, 4 as West African organized crime task forces, 9 as electronic crimes task forces, and 1 as a violent crimes task force. According to Secret Service officials, investigations conducted by each the 38 task forces can include identity theft-related cases, although none of the 38 focuses solely or exclusively on such cases.

According to the Secret Service, electronic crimes task forces concentrate on crimes involving e-commerce, telecommunications fraud, and computer intrusions (hacking), as well as cases involving missing and exploited children. An identity theft-related example is an investigation initiated in December 2000 by the electronic crimes task force of the Secret Service's New York Field Office. According to Secret Service testimony presented in May 2001 at a congressional hearing:[15]

- The investigation, which was conducted jointly by the Secret Service and the New York Police Department, determined that the credit card accounts of many of the nation's wealthiest chief executive officers, as well as many other citizens, had been compromised.
- Using the Internet and cellular telephones, the perpetrators obtained the victims' credit card account numbers and then established fictitious addresses to conduct fraudulent transactions.
- Also, the perpetrators attempted to transfer approximately $22 million—from the legitimate brokerage and corporate accounts of the victims—into fraudulently established accounts for conversion to the perpetrators' own use.

Table 3 presents an example of another Secret Service electronic crimes task force, which was first developed in 1995 by the agency's Washington (District of Columbia) Field Office and has subsequently grown to include a total of 32 participating law enforcement agencies and private sector entities.

Secret Service officials said that the agency's task forces generate cases that result in prosecutions in state and local courts as well as in federal courts. The officials estimated, for instance, that the majority (about 60 percent) of the Washington Field Office Task Force's cases had been prosecuted in state courts. Further, regarding the operations of Secret Service task forces in general, the officials noted that, while the Secret Service may have overall administrative responsibility, the role of "quarterback" regarding the investigative agenda often is a shared role. In explanation, the officials said that the task forces do get involved in cases important to the needs of local communities.

---

[15] Prepared statement of Mr. Bruce Townsend, Special Agent in Charge, Financial Crimes Division, U.S. Secret Service, for a hearing ("On-line Fraud and Crime: Are Consumers Safe?") before the Subcommittee on Commerce, Trade, and Consumer Protection; House Committee on Energy and Commerce (May 23, 2001).

Table 3: Participants in Electronic Crimes Task Force Developed by Secret Service's Washington Field Office

Task force participants	Number of agencies or entities
Federal law enforcement agencies: Bureau of Alcohol, Tobacco and Firearms; Customs Service; Defense Criminal Investigative Service; Department of Housing and Urban Development; Department of State; Drug Enforcement Administration; FBI; General Services Administration; Immigration and Naturalization Service; Metropolitan Washington Airports Authority; Postal Inspection Service; Secret Service; and SSA.	13
State and local law enforcement agencies: Bladensburg Police Department, Hyattsville Police Department, Fairfax County Police Department, Maryland State Police, Metropolitan Police Department, Montgomery County Police Department, Mount Rainier Police Department, Prince George's County Police Department, and Vienna Police Department.	9
Private sector entities: Allfirst Bank, Bank of America, Bell Atlantic, Cellular One, Chevy Chase Bank, Citibank, First Union Bank, MBNA, Target Department Stores, and Wachovia Bank.	10
Total number of law enforcement agencies and private sector entities	**32**

Source: Secret Service.

California: High-Technology Task Forces Address Identity Theft

In the mid-1990s, the California Attorney General's Office established five regional task forces in the state to facilitate multi-jurisdictional investigations and prosecutions of high-technology crimes, such as the theft of chips and other computer components. The five high-technology task forces also are to address identity theft/fraud and its related crimes. One of the five is the Sacramento Valley High-Technology Crime Task Force, which was reorganized in October 1999 as a separate division within the Sacramento County Sheriff's Department. The task force includes participants from local, state, and federal agencies in the 34 counties of the eastern judicial district of the state of California. As of calendar year 2001, a total of 32 agencies or entities were represented, as table 4 shows.

Table 4: Participants in the Sacramento Valley High-Technology Crimes Task Force

Task force participants	Number of agencies or entities
Police departments: Davis, Folsom, Modesto, Isleton, Roseville, Sacramento, Turlock, West Sacramento, and Yuba.	9
Sheriff's departments: El Dorado, Merced, Placer, Sacramento, San Joaquin, Stanislaus, Sutter, and Tuolumne.	8
District attorney offices: Placer, Sacramento, and Yolo.	3
State agencies: Controller's Office, Department of Corrections, Department of Justice, Department of Motor Vehicles, Highway Patrol, Probation (Sacramento), and University of California (Davis).	7
Federal agencies: FBI, Forest Service, Postal Inspection Service, Secret Service, and U.S. Attorney's Office.	5
Total number of agencies and entities	**32**

Source: Sacramento Valley High-Technology Crimes Task Force.

According to its annual report for calendar year 2001, the Sacramento Valley High-Technology Crimes Task Force investigated 153 cases involving identity theft. Examples of these cases included the following:

- Detectives were called to the Sacramento International Airport to investigate a suspect who used stolen credit card information to purchase tickets for two other suspects. The investigation revealed 24 other victims whose credit cards had been stolen by one of the suspects from his place of employment.

- A suspect attempted to purchase items at a store using a manufactured fraudulent check. After being arrested, the suspect identified herself using another person's identity and was booked into jail using that name. However, an investigation determined the suspect's true identity and that she had written at least seven other fraudulent checks in the Sacramento area.

- A suspect used a victim's identity to open an account at a jewelry store and charge several items. Also, the suspect opened several other accounts in the victim's name and made purchases (some over the Internet) using these accounts. Further, the investigation found numerous names, credit information, SSNs, and driver's licenses—and documents with Internet Web sites, passwords, and personal identification numbers—indicating that the suspect had opened accounts using the personal information of the victims.

Florida: Statewide Initiative to Investigate and Prosecute Identity Theft Cases

Identity theft-related enforcement efforts in Florida are being led by the Florida Attorney General's Office of Statewide Prosecution and the Florida Department of Law Enforcement. In 2001, these agencies partnered to create a statewide task force initiative to target perpetrators of identity fraud. The initiative—called Operation LEGIT (law enforcement getting identity thieves)—has special agents and other personnel assigned from various regional offices of the Florida Department of Law Enforcement. Other task force participants can include local and federal law enforcement agencies, as indicated in the following examples of cases:[16]

- For more than 12 years, a Florida suspect assumed and lived under the identity of a California victim, who had lost his wallet (with his driver's license and other personal identification information) while vacationing in Daytona Beach in 1987. Since that time, the suspect had purchased and sold homes, opened bank accounts, obtained credit, established utility and phone service, and been arrested on at least three separate occasions. Based on a Florida warrant, the victim was wrongly arrested in California and held in jail for more than a week. Also, the victim has had civil judgments levied against him. The investigation that led to the suspect's arrest was initiated in May 2001 and was conducted by the Hernando County (Florida) Sheriff's Office, the Florida Department of Law Enforcement, the Office of Statewide Prosecution, and SSA/OIG.

- In July 2001, six suspects were charged with racketeering and multiple counts of identity theft that affected victims throughout Florida. The ringleader orchestrated the scheme from a Florida prison (Gulf County Correctional Facility), where he was serving a 9-year sentence for his involvement in a similar investigation that concluded in 1998, with victims throughout Florida and Georgia. Using the inmate telephone system and the U.S. mail service, the ringleader obtained account and identity information of unsuspecting consumers. Accomplices used the compromised identities to commit credit card fraud, purchase vehicles, open fraudulent checking accounts, and apply for instant loans at furniture stores and other businesses across Florida. The organized scheme netted the ring more than $200,000 in stolen property. This case was investigated by the Florida Department of Law Enforcement, the Office of Statewide Prosecution, and SSA/OIG.

---

[16] The examples are excerpts from news releases made by Florida's Office of Statewide Prosecution. Generally, the news releases noted that charges are merely accusations and arrested defendants are presumed innocent until and unless the charges are proven beyond a reasonable doubt.

- In October 2001, six suspects were arrested for fraudulently obtaining nearly $300,000 in merchandise, after assuming the identities of 18 individuals from around the country. An employee of a children's clinic in Orlando obtained the SSNs and other identifying information of the 18 individuals, who had participated in a medical study concerning cystic fibrosis and whose children suffer from the disease. The employee passed the information to another person, who created false birth certificates and other documents that were used to obtain identity cards in the names of the victims through offices of the Florida Department of Motor Vehicles. The suspects used the false identities to obtain instant credit at electronic and furniture stores in Orange and Seminole Counties in Florida. The suspects purchased big-screen televisions, computers, and other high-cost items until the victims' credit lines were exhausted. The purchased items were later sold on the streets of Orlando (Florida) and Chicago (Illinois) for half their retail value, with the proceeds divided by the suspects. The investigation was conducted by the Orlando Police Department, the Florida Department of Law Enforcement, and the Office of Statewide Prosecution.

- In February 2002, a former resident of Daytona Beach was charged with obtaining personal identifying information (names, addresses, and SSNs) on various individuals and using the information to fraudulently purchase more than $35,000 worth of merchandise throughout east-central Florida. The suspect obtained the information from a Web site used legitimately by a variety of businesses and individuals for the purpose of finding and tracking others. As of February 2002, the then-ongoing investigation by the Florida Department of Law Enforcement revealed that the suspect had compromised the identities of victims in 12 states.

Identity Theft Subcommittee Formed to Have Coordination and Education Role

In early 1999, following passage of the federal Identity Theft Act in 1998, the U.S. Attorney General's Council on White Collar Crime established the Subcommittee on Identity Theft to foster coordination of investigative and prosecutorial strategies and promote consumer education programs. Subcommittee leadership is vested in the Fraud Section of the Department of Justice's Criminal Division, and membership includes various federal law enforcement and regulatory agencies, as well as state and local representation through the International Association of Chiefs of Police, the National Association of Attorneys General, and the National District Attorneys Association.

In response to our inquiries, the Chairman of the subcommittee said that, although there is no written charter or mission statement, the role and activities of the subcommittee are substantially as follows:

- Initially, to promote awareness and use of the federal Identity Theft Act, the subcommittee prepared guidance memorandums for field distribution to law enforcement and regulatory agencies. Also, the subcommittee helped to plan or support various identity theft-related educational presentations and workshops, with participants from the public and private sectors.

- Because so much of identity theft is a local matter, it was imperative that the subcommittee's membership include state and local representatives. Participation by the International Association of Chiefs of Police gives the subcommittee a channel to thousands of local law enforcement entities. A continuing priority of the subcommittee is to help educate local police departments about the critical first step of taking reports from victims of identity theft crime.

- Furthermore, the subcommittee continually promotes the availability of FTC's Consumer Sentinel Network as a tool for federal, state, and local law enforcement agencies to use.

The subcommittee Chairman also noted that, since the terrorist incidents of September 11, 2001, there has been more of a focus on prevention. For example, the American Association of Motor Vehicle Administrators attended a recent subcommittee meeting to discuss ways to protect against counterfeit or fake driver's licenses.

To obtain a broader understanding of the subcommittee's role, as well as ways to potentially enhance that role, we contacted the designated individuals who, respectively, represented six member organizations—FBI, National District Attorneys Association, Postal Inspection Service, Secret Service, Sentencing Commission, and SSA/OIG. Generally, the representatives commented that the subcommittee has been helpful in combating identity theft and has been functioning well, particularly considering the fact that membership is a collateral duty for each representative. One member—representing the National District Attorneys Association—suggested that the subcommittee's role could be enhanced by having a formal charter or mission statement detailing each participant's role. However, the FBI and Secret Service representatives said that the informality of the subcommittee promotes member participation and also commented that additional directives could be counterproductive.

Opportunities for Law Enforcement to Use FTC Data to Aid in Investigations of Identity Theft

Since its establishment in 1999, FTC's Identity Theft Data Clearinghouse has been used for reporting statistical and demographic information about victims and perpetrators. While not immediate, the value of the Clearinghouse database as a law enforcement tool has been growing but has not reached its full potential. In conducting investigations, for example, relatively few law enforcement agencies have used FTC's Consumer Sentinel Network, which provides computer access to the Clearinghouse database. Further, centralized analysis of database information to generate investigative leads and referrals has been limited. Law enforcement's limited use of the Consumer Sentinel Network and the Clearinghouse database may be due to various reasons, including the relatively short operating history of the database. To promote greater awareness and use of the Network and the Clearinghouse database, FTC and Secret Service outreach efforts include conducting regional law enforcement training seminars and developing a training video for distribution to local law enforcement agencies across the nation.

FTC Established the Identity Theft Data Clearinghouse in 1999

The federal Identity Theft Act of 1998 required FTC to "log and acknowledge the receipt of complaints by individuals who certify that they have a reasonable belief" that one or more of their means of identification have been assumed, stolen, or otherwise unlawfully acquired. In response to this requirement, in November 1999, FTC established the Identity Theft Data Clearinghouse to gather information from any consumer who wishes to file a complaint or pose an inquiry concerning identity theft. Consumers can call a toll-free telephone number (1-877-ID-THEFT) to report identity theft. Information from complainants is accumulated in a central database (the Identity Theft Data Clearinghouse) for use as an aid in law enforcement and prevention of identity theft. From its establishment in November 1999 through September 2001, the Clearinghouse received a total of 94,100 complaints from identity theft victims. This total includes 16,784 complaints transferred to the FTC from the SSA/OIG. In the first month of operation, the Clearinghouse answered an average of 445 calls per week. By March 2001, the average number of calls had increased to over 2,000 per week. In December 2001, the weekly average was about 3,000 answered calls.

From its inception, the Clearinghouse database has been used to report statistical and demographic information about victims and perpetrators. For example, regarding identity theft complaints received in calendar year 2001, an FTC official testifying at a

March 2002 congressional hearing summarized database information partly as follows:[17]

> "The Clearinghouse database has been in operation for more than two years. ... While not comprehensive, information from the database can reveal information about the nature of identity theft activity. For example, the data show that California has the greatest overall number of victims in the FTC's database, followed by New York, Texas, Florida, and Illinois. On a per capita basis, per 100,000 citizens, the District of Columbia ranks first, followed by California, Nevada, Maryland and New York. The cities with the highest numbers of victims reporting to the database are New York, Chicago, Los Angeles, Houston, and Miami.
>
> "Eighty-eight percent of victims reporting to the FTC provide their age. The largest number of these victims (28%) were in their thirties. The next largest group includes consumers from age eighteen to twenty-nine (26%), followed by consumers in their forties (22%). Consumers in their fifties comprised 13%, and those age 60 and over comprised 9%. Minors under 18 years of age comprised 2% of victims....
>
> "Thirty-five percent of the victims had not yet notified any credit bureau at the time they contacted the FTC; 46% had not yet notified any of the financial institutions involved. Fifty-four percent of the victims had not yet notified their local police department of the identity theft. By advising the callers to take these critical steps, we enable many victims to get through the recovery process more efficiently and effectively."

Centralized Analysis of Clearinghouse Data to Generate Investigative Leads and Referrals is Increasing

In addition to providing a basis for reporting statistical and demographic information about identity theft victims and perpetrators, another primary purpose of the Clearinghouse database is to support law enforcement. Since May 2001, one Secret Service special agent, working with an FTC attorney, an investigator, and a paralegal, has been involved in centrally analyzing Clearinghouse data to generate investigative leads and referrals. Specifically, according to FTC staff:

- The team uses intelligence software to analyze Clearinghouse data to generate investigative leads.
- These leads are then further developed using criminal investigative resources provided by the Secret Service and research and analytical tools provided by the FTC.

---

[17] Prepared statement of the FTC, *Identity Theft: the FTC's Response*, before the Subcommittee on Technology, Terrorism and Government Information, Senate Judiciary Committee (Mar. 20, 2002).

- When the case leads have been comprehensively developed, they are referred to federal, state, or local law enforcement officers in the field. These officers participate in financial, high-tech, or economic crimes task forces and are well equipped to handle the cases.

The pace of developing and sending out investigative leads has picked up since FTC and the Secret Service jointly initiated their efforts in May 2001. For instance, 10 investigative referrals were made to regional law enforcement during the last 6 months of calendar year 2001, whereas 19 referrals were made in the first 5 months of 2002. One of the 29 referrals involved 10 individuals with the same address. In response to our inquiries in May 2002, Secret Service officials said that the 29 referrals were still being worked and, thus, the results or outcomes were yet to be determined.

Relatively Few Law Enforcement Agencies Use the Consumer Sentinel Network to Access FTC's Identity Theft Data Clearinghouse

In addition to receiving referrals based on centralized analysis of Clearinghouse data, federal, state, and local law enforcement agencies nationwide can use desktop computers to access Clearinghouse data to further support ongoing cases or develop new leads. Specifically, through FTC's Consumer Sentinel Network—which is a secure, encrypted Web site—law enforcement agencies can access Clearinghouse data and use search tools tailored for identity theft investigations. For instance, an investigator may scan consumer complaints matching certain criteria to determine if there is a larger pattern of criminal activity. FTC does not charge a fee for use of the Consumer Sentinel Network. However, each law enforcement agency must enter into a confidentiality agreement (pledging to abide by applicable confidentiality rules) with FTC.

As of May 24, 2002, a total of 46 federal agencies had signed user agreements with FTC, facilitating access to Identity Theft Data Clearinghouse information via the Consumer Sentinel Network. These agencies include the FBI, Secret Service, Postal Inspection Service, SSA/OIG, and some U. S. Attorney Offices. Further, relatively few of the nation's over 18,000 state and local law enforcement agencies have signed agreements with FTC to use the Consumer Sentinel Network to access the Identity Theft Data Clearinghouse. Specifically, as of May 24, 2002, a total of 306 state and local law enforcement agencies had entered into such agreements. Of this total, the number of users varied from 1 law enforcement agency in each of 5 states (Delaware, Hawaii, Idaho, New Hampshire, and New Mexico) and 2 agencies in each of 8 other states (Arizona, Arkansas, Kansas, Massachusetts, Nebraska, Oregon, South Dakota, and Wyoming) to 17 agencies in Texas and 45 agencies in California. Even at the high end of this range, the extent of access is not comprehensive. For example:

- In Texas, the Houston Police Department and the Harris County Sheriff's Office—jurisdictions that encompass about 22 percent of the state's population—are not users of the Consumer Sentinel Network. As stated previously, in reference to number of identity theft victims, Houston is among the top five cities nationally. Overall, less than 1 percent of the state's law enforcement agencies have entered into confidentiality agreements with FTC.

- Although California has the largest number of users (45 agencies), the list of subscribers does not include the city police departments in Los Angeles, Sacramento, or San Jose. As mentioned previously, over 8,000 cases of identity theft were reported to the Los Angeles Police Department in calendar year 2001.

According to FTC staff, the number of Consumer Sentinel member agencies continually increases, particularly in response to outreach activities such as regional law enforcement training.

FTC staff provided us query statistics showing external law enforcement usage of the Consumer Sentinel Network and the Identity Theft Data Clearinghouse for January 2001 through March 2002. During this 15-month period, the number of external law enforcement queries about identity theft complaints totaled 7,946—an average of about 530 per month—and ranged from 378 in December 2001 to 783 in January 2002. FTC staff noted that these usage statistics do not reflect centralized analysis of identity theft complaint data, conducted jointly by the Secret Service and FTC.

Reasons for Limited Law Enforcement Use of Consumer Sentinel Network and Clearinghouse Database

Various reasons may explain law enforcement's relatively limited use of the Consumer Sentinel Network and the Identity Theft Data Clearinghouse database. Department of Justice officials said, for instance, that many state and local agencies may have an insufficient number of computers and support personnel, in addition to being challenged by competing priorities. Also, FTC staff and Secret Service officials noted that the availability of the Clearinghouse database as an aid for law enforcement agencies is still relatively new. As such, some potential users are unaware of this investigative resource, despite ongoing outreach efforts.

Further, regarding usefulness of database information for law enforcement purposes, we asked whether any examples of federal, state, or local success stories had been presented or discussed at any of the monthly meetings of the Attorney General's Identity Theft Subcommittee. In response, the head of the subcommittee told us that none of the meetings had included such examples—neither examples involving field agencies that used the Consumer Sentinel Network to develop cases nor examples involving the results of investigative leads or referrals that were based on centralized analysis of Clearinghouse data.

One state's deputy attorney general, in replying to our inquiry about the usefulness of the Consumer Sentinel Network and the Clearinghouse database, said that, as a practical matter, a local investigator with numerous outstanding cases on his or her desk will not be using the FTC system to obtain more cases. Rather, this state official suggested, for example, that FTC could use the system to generate periodic reports to alert law enforcement of specific problems within their respective jurisdictions and facilitate the coordination of investigative resources for the maximum benefit.

FTC staff acknowledged that Sentinel members appear to use the Clearinghouse database to bolster the cases they have under investigation more often than to initiate new cases. However, the FTC staff told us that they are continuously looking for ways to make the Clearinghouse database more efficient and user friendly. The staff noted, for example, that FTC has established an e-mail address to take requests for specific searches from Sentinel members and, thereby, FTC can use its internal search tools to query the Clearinghouse database and provide more comprehensive results to requesters. Also, the staff noted that FTC expects to implement an "alert" function before the end of fiscal year 2002. According to the staff:

- The alert function will enable a Clearinghouse user (e.g., police officer) to flag or annotate one or more particular complaints relating to an investigation that the user is conducting. If and when another user executes a query that retrieves one of the flagged complaints, this second user will get a pop-up message box asking him or her to contact the first user before proceeding.

- Thus, two police officers, who likely are from different jurisdictions but are looking at the same complaint records, can avoid duplicating investigatory efforts or inadvertently impeding each other's investigations.

Also, the staff noted that FTC has plans to implement (by the end of fiscal year 2002) a report listing the suspect locations most frequently reported in the database.[18] Further, in response to requests from Sentinel members, the FTC will soon begin testing a program to provide Sentinel members access to electronic batches of Clearinghouse data—for example, all complaint information reported by victims in a given city during a specified period of time. According to FTC staff, Sentinel members will be able to run the batched data through their own intelligence or link

---

[18] Further, as discussed in appendix V, FTC and the Department of Defense have agreed to establish Soldier Sentinel, an online system designed specifically to collect consumer and identity theft complaint information from members of the armed forces and their families.

analysis software and also combine the data with their own investigative information for more impact.

Moreover, FTC staff said that additional steps are being taken to increase law enforcement agencies' awareness and use of the Consumer Sentinel Network and the Clearinghouse database. The staff noted, for example, that training sessions for law enforcement agencies were conducted in Washington, D.C., in March 2002, in Des Moines, Iowa, and Chicago, Illinois, in May 2002, and that additional sessions are planned for San Francisco, California, in June 2002, and for Dallas, Texas, in August 2002. Also, as mentioned previously, the Secret Service is developing a police training video with the cooperation of the FTC, Department of Justice, and the International Association of Chiefs of Police, which is anticipated to be completed by September 30, 2002. According to FTC staff and Secret Service officials, the training video will briefly discuss the availability of the Consumer Sentinel Network and the Identity Theft Data Clearinghouse, in addition to emphasizing the importance of police reports in identity theft cases.

These planned initiatives appear to be steps in the right direction. If implemented effectively, the initiatives should help to ensure that more law enforcement agencies are aware of existing data that can be used to combat identity theft. Nonetheless, concerted and continued outreach efforts will be needed to promote broad awareness and use of the Consumer Sentinel Network and the Clearinghouse database by all levels of law enforcement.

SSA/OIG ACTIONS TO RESOLVE SSN MISUSE AND OTHER IDENTITY THEFT-RELATED ALLEGATIONS

As mentioned previously, SSA/OIG's fraud hotline annually receives tens of thousands of allegations, most of which involve either (1) SSN misuse or (2) program fraud with SSN misuse potential. In these 2 categories, SSA/OIG received approximately 62,000 allegations in fiscal year 1999, and the agency opened investigative cases on 4,636 (about 7 percent) of these allegations. About three in four of the investigative cases involved program fraud-related allegations. Generally, SSA/OIG concentrates its investigative resources on this category of allegations because the protection of Social Security trust funds is a priority. SSA/OIG statistics for investigative cases opened in fiscal year 1999 indicate that a total of 1,347 cases had resulted in criminal convictions or other judicial actions, as of April 30, 2002. During our review, the SSA Inspector General told us that his office does not have enough investigators to address all of the SSN misuse allegations received on the agency's fraud hotline. However, FTC staff noted that, starting in February 2001, FTC began to routinely upload information from SSA/OIG's fraud hotline about these allegations into FTC's Identity Theft Data Clearinghouse, thereby making the information available to law enforcement agencies via the Consumer Sentinel Network.

SSA/OIG Concentrates Its Investigative Resources on Allegations of Program Fraud with SSN Misuse Potential

Within the categories of SSN misuse and program fraud with SSN misuse potential, SSA/OIG received a total of 62,376 allegations in fiscal year 1999, a greater number (83,721) in fiscal year 2000, and an even higher number (104,103) in fiscal year 2001. According to SSA/OIG officials, allegations are reviewed by supervisory personnel to determine which should be further pursued. The review criteria, among others, include considerations of the credibility of the alleged information, the actual or potential dollar-loss amounts involved, the severity of other effects on SSA programs, and the prosecutive merits of the allegation, as well as considerations of current workloads and the availability of investigative resources.

Most allegations of identity theft made to SSA/OIG do not result in criminal investigations being opened. Of the two categories of allegations, however, SSA/OIG generally concentrates its investigative resources on allegations of program fraud with SSN misuse potential because the protection of Social Security trust funds is a priority. In fiscal year 1999, for example, SSA/OIG opened investigative cases on 12 percent of the allegations categorized as program fraud with SSN misuse potential and 3 percent of the allegations categorized as SSN misuse (see table 5). In other words, although the total numbers of allegations received in each category were similar, program fraud-related allegations were about four times more likely to result in investigative cases being opened.

Table 5: Allegations Received by SSA/OIG and Investigative Cases Opened, Fiscal Year 1999

Allegation type	Number of allegations received	Number of investigative cases opened	Percentage of allegations investigated
SSN misuse	30,116	868	3
Program fraud with SSN misuse potential	32,260	3,768	12
Total	**62,376**	**4,636**	**7**

Source: SSA/OIG data.

Investigations of Allegations Have Produced Convictions and Other Judicial Actions

In response to our inquiry regarding the results of SSA/OIG criminal investigations, the agency provided us statistics for applicable cases opened in fiscal year 1999 that resulted in criminal or other judicial actions. As table 6 shows, as of April 30, 2002, SSN misuse cases (768) accounted for 57 percent of the 1,347 investigations involving SSN misuse or program fraud with SSN misuse potential that were opened in fiscal year 1999 and resulted in criminal or other judicial actions.

Table 6: Results, as of April 30, 2002, of SSA/OIG Investigations Opened in Fiscal Year 1999

Results category	Description of category	Number of investigations resulting in criminal or other judicial actions			Percentage of total number
		SSN misuse	Program fraud with SSN misuse potential	Total	
Individual convicted and sentenced	These cases involved accused individuals who were tried, found guilty, and sentenced.	338	339	677	50
Alien apprehended and deported	These cases involved the taking into custody of an illegal alien or undocumented immigrant, who used the SSN of another person.	423	31	454	34
Fugitive felon apprehended	These cases involved individuals who were receiving Social Security benefits and who were also the subjects of outstanding warrants. SSA/OIG coordinated with the U.S. Marshals Service or state or local law enforcement to apprehend the fugitive.	0	137	137	10
First-time offender handled by pretrial diversion program	These cases involved first-time offenders who were placed on probation for 12 to 18 months.	7	72	79	6
Total		768	579	1,347	100
Percentage of total		57	43	100	

Note: Data represent criminal investigations that were opened in fiscal year 1999 by SSA/OIG and that were closed with a criminal or other judicial actions as of April 30, 2002. Other criminal investigations may have resulted in civil monetary penalties or administrative action or may have been closed with no action.

Source: SSA/OIG data.

SSA/OIG officials said that investigations of SSN misuse allegations produce convictions or other criminal results because SSN misuse generally is tied to other white-collar or financial crimes that can have identity theft-related elements. On the other hand, the officials said that many investigations of program fraud cases may be closed with administrative actions, which can include suspension of benefit payments.

SSA/OIG Allegation Information is Now Being Added to FTC's Database

In recent years, the number of SSN misuse allegations received by the SSA/OIG has grown faster than the number of program fraud-related allegations. That is, SSN misuse allegations constitute a growing proportion of these two categories of allegations, increasing from 48 percent in fiscal year 1999, to 56 percent in fiscal year 2000, and to 63 percent in fiscal year 2001. During our review, the SSA Inspector General told us that, given limited resources and competing priorities, his office investigates relatively few allegations of SSN misuse. Consequently, the Inspector General said that many credible allegations of identity theft that have the potential to produce criminal convictions or other judicial actions are not addressed.

Starting in February 2001, FTC began routinely uploading SSA/OIG information about SSN misuse allegations into FTC's Identity Theft Data Clearinghouse. This enhancement of the Clearinghouse database makes the SSA/OIG allegation information available to law enforcement agencies via the Consumer Sentinel Network. However, as discussed previously, relatively few law enforcement agencies use the Network, and centralized analysis of Clearinghouse data to generate investigative leads and referrals has been limited.

CONCLUSIONS

Comprehensive results—such as number of prosecutions and convictions—under the federal Identity Theft Act and relevant state statutes are not available. However, examples of actual cases illustrate that identity theft often is a component of other white-collar or financial crimes, and these cases often have fact-pattern elements involving more than one jurisdiction. Moreover, the prevalence of identity theft and the frequently multi- or cross-jurisdictional nature of such crimes underscore the importance of leveraging available resources and promoting cooperation or coordination among all levels of law enforcement.

Our review indicates that there are opportunities for law enforcement to make greater use of existing data to combat identity theft. In particular, the Consumer Sentinel Network potentially can provide all law enforcement agencies across the nation with access to FTC's Identity Theft Data Clearinghouse database to support ongoing investigations. In addition to complaint information reported by identity theft victims directly to FTC, the Clearinghouse database now routinely incorporates identity theft-related information received by SSA/OIG. However, despite outreach efforts to date, relatively few state and local law enforcement agencies have signed Consumer Sentinel confidentiality agreements with FTC. Also, although the number is increasing, few investigative leads and referrals have been generated by centralized analysis of database information. Given the growing prevalence of identity theft, continued and concerted emphasis is warranted regarding the availability and use of the Consumer Sentinel Network and the Clearinghouse database as law enforcement tools.

APPENDIX: EXAMPLES OF CASES PROSECUTED UNDER THE FEDERAL IDENTITY THEFT ACT

This appendix summarizes selected federal cases prosecuted under the Identity Theft and Assumption Deterrence Act of 1998. The relevant section of this legislation is codified at 18 U.S.C. § 1028(a)(7)("fraud and related activity in connection with identification documents and information"). The cases summarized in this appendix are not intended to be a comprehensive listing of all federal prosecutions under the 1998 federal statute. We identified these cases by conducting a search of the LexisNexis database in February 2002. Our search was designed to retrieve only those identity theft cases that specifically mentioned the federal statute—that is, cases that cited 18 U.S.C. § 1028(a)(7).

The following summaries of five cases prosecuted in U.S. district courts illustrate that identity theft generally is not a stand-alone crime. Rather, identity theft typically is a component of one or more other white-collar or financial crimes, such as bank fraud, credit card or access device fraud, or mail fraud.

Illinois, Northern District, Eastern Division

In early 2001, a defendant was charged in a six-count indictment with bank fraud (counts 1, 2, and 3), possession of a counterfeit check (count 4), interstate transportation of a counterfeit check (count 5), and use of another person's SSN with intent to commit a state felony (count 6). In May 2001, the defendant pleaded guilty to counts 1 and 6 pursuant to a written plea agreement, and the remaining counts were dismissed. The district court sentenced the defendant to concurrent 46-month prison terms for offense conduct under the Identity Theft Act, 18 U.S.C. § 1028(a)(7)—using another person's SSN with intent to commit a crime—and under 18 U.S.C. § 1344 (bank fraud). *U.S. v. Burks*, No. 01-3313, 2002 U.S. App. Lexis 2387 (7th Cir. Feb. 11, 2002).

Michigan, Western District, Southern Division

This was a consolidated case involving three separate actions, in which three plaintiffs each alleged liability against the defendant car dealership, whose salesman/employee committed criminal acts. Specifically, the salesman/employee wrongly obtained credit reports for the plaintiffs, without their consent, and then used the reports to secure financing for car sales or leases for applicants with bad credit histories. The salesman/employee was convicted on a federal fraud criminal charge under 18 U.S.C. § 1028(a)(7). Also, the plaintiffs established liability against the dealership for intentional violation of the Fair Credit Reporting Act. *Benjamin Adams v. Berger Chevrolet, Inc.*, No. 1:00-CV-225, 1:00-CV-226, and 1:00-CV-228, 2001 Dist. Lexis 6174 (W.D. Mich. May 7, 2001).

North Carolina, Eastern District

A defendant was charged with stealing mail from residential mailboxes, using information from personal checks to create counterfeit checks and fraudulent driver's licenses, and negotiating the counterfeit checks at numerous banks in North Carolina using the fraudulent licenses as identification. The defendant pled guilty to

- one count of using false identification documents, 18 U.S.C. § 1028(a)(7);
- five counts of producing false identification documents, 18 U.S.C. § 1028(a)(1); and
- three counts of possession of stolen mail, 18 U.S.C. § 1708.

The defendant was sentenced to a term of 63 months of imprisonment. *U.S. v. Hooks*, No. 99-4754, 2000 U.S. App. Lexis 2388 (4th Cir. Sept. 14, 2000).

Ohio, Southern District

In May 2000, following a bench trial, the district court found a defendant guilty of the following violations

- using the identification of another with intent to commit unlawful activity, 18 U.S.C. § 1028(a)(7);

- possessing false identification with intent to defraud the United States, 18 U.S.C. § 1028(a)(4);
- furnishing false information to the Commissioner of Social Security, 42 U.S.C. § 408(a)(6);
- fraud and misuse of an entry document, 18 U.S.C. § 1546, and
- making a false statement to an agency of the United States, 18 U.S.C. § 1001.

The court sentenced the defendant to 6 months of imprisonment, plus 3 years of supervised release. *U.S. v. Balde*, No. 00-4070, 2001 U.S. App. Lexis 23741 (6th Cir. Oct. 26, 2001).

Wisconsin, Eastern District

A defendant pleaded guilty to using another person's SSN to commit fraud, 18 U.S.C. § 1028(a)(7); using unauthorized credit cards, 18 U.S.C. § 1029(a)(2); and issuing a false SSN, 42 U.S.C. § 408(a)(7)(B).

The defendant was sentenced to 36 months of imprisonment. *U.S. v. Lippold*, No. 00-2868, 2001 U.S. App. Lexis 15126 (7th Cir. July 2, 2001).

Chapter 6

IDENTITY THEFT AND THE FAIR CREDIT REPORTING ACT: AN ANALYSIS OF *TRW V. ANDREWS* AND CURRENT LEGISLATION[*]

Angie A. Welborn

INTRODUCTION

One of the ways in which victims of identity theft may recover for financial harm is by filing suit under the Fair Credit Reporting Act.[1] However, the Act imposes a two year statute of limitations on suits filed. On November 13, 2001, the Supreme Court decided a case interpreting when the Act's statute of limitations begins to run. In that case, the Court held that the statute of limitations begins to run when inaccurate disclosures first occur, and not when the consumer learns of the inaccuracies in his report.

Several pieces of legislation attempting to provide consumers with additional time to file suit have been introduced in response to the Court's decision. This chapter will provide a brief summary of the Fair Credit Reporting Act provisions in question, as well as an analysis of the recent Supreme Court decision and an overview of recent legislation (S. 22 and H.R. 818) introduced in response to that decision.

---

[*] Excerpted from CRS Report RS21083. Updated March 21, 2003.
[1] For more information on remedies available to victims of identity theft, see CRS Report RS21163, *Remedies Available to Victims of Identity Theft*.

FAIR CREDIT REPORTING ACT

The Fair Credit Reporting Act (FCRA) was enacted on October 26, 1970.[2] The purpose of the FCRA is "to require that consumer reporting agencies adopt reasonable procedures for meeting the needs of commerce for consumer credit, personnel, insurance, and other information in a manner which is fair and equitable to the consumer, with regard to the confidentiality, accuracy, relevancy, and proper utilization of such information."[3] The FCRA applies to the files maintained by "consumer reporting agencies," a term broadly defined to include anyone in the business of furnishing reports on the credit worthiness of consumers to third parties.[4] Consumer credit reports generally include information about a consumer's "credit worthiness, credit standing, credit capacity, character, general reputation, personal characteristics, or mode of living."[5] This information is gathered and sold to creditors, employers, landlords and other businesses. The FCRA outlines a consumer's rights in relation to his or her credit report, as well as permissible uses for credit reports and disclosure requirements. In addition, the FCRA requires credit reporting agencies to follow "reasonable procedures to assure maximum possible accuracy of the information concerning the individual about whom the report relates."[6]

The FCRA allows consumers to file suit for violations of the Act, which could include the disclosure of inaccurate information about a consumer by a credit reporting agency.[7] A consumer who is a victim of identity theft could file suit against a credit reporting agency for the agency's failure to verify the accuracy of information contained in the report and the agency's disclosure of inaccurate information as a result of the consumer's stolen identity. Generally, the FCRA requires consumer to file suit "within two years from the date on which the liability arises."[8] However, there is an exception in cases where there was willful misrepresentation of information that is required to be disclosed to a consumer and such information is material to the establishment of the defendant's liability.[9] In such cases, the action

---

[2] P.L. 91-508, tit. 6, § 601, 84 *Stat.* 1128, 15 U.S.C. 1681 *et. seq.* For more information on the Fair Credit Reporting Act, see CRS Report RL31666, *Fair Credit Reporting Act: Rights and Responsibilities.*
[3] 15 U.S.C. 1681(b).
[4] 15 U.S.C. 1681a(f).
[5] 15 U.S.C. 1681a(d). In addition to credit information, consumer reporting agencies are allowed to include information on the failure of the consumer to pay overdue child support, if such information has been provided to the agency by a state or local child support enforcement agency or verified by any state or federal government agency. This information remains on the consumer report for up to 7 years. 15 U.S.C. 1681s-1.
[6] 15 U.S.C. 1681e(b).
[7] 15 U.S.C. 1681n; 15 U.S.C. 1681o.
[8] 15 U.S.C. 1681p.
[9] *Id.*

"may be brought any time within two years after the discovery by the individual of the misrepresentation."[10]

TRW v. Andrews

The plaintiff in *TRW v. Andrews* was a victim of identity theft.[11] An imposter, who had the same last name and first initial as the plaintiff, obtained Andrews' social security number and attempted to open numerous credit accounts under the imposter's name. On four occasions, the creditors responding to the impostor's applications sought reports from TRW, a credit reporting agency. TRW matched the social security number, last name, and first initial with Andrews' file and disclosed her credit history to the creditors.

Andrews did not learn of the disclosures until she attempted to refinance her home and requested a copy of her credit report, which reflected the impostor's activity. TRW corrected Andrews' file when notified of the mistakes. However, Andrews alleged that the blemishes on her credit report "forced her to abandon her refinancing efforts and settle for an alternative line of credit on less favorable terms."[12]

Andrews filed suit against TRW on October 21, 1996, approximately 17 months after she became aware of the inaccurate information on her credit report and more than two years after TRW made the two initial disclosures.[13] Andrews alleged that TRW's failure to verify, prior to disclosing information to creditors, that she initiated the requests or was otherwise involved in the underlying transactions was in violation of the Fair Credit Reporting Act's requirement that credit reporting agencies maintain reasonable procedures to avoid improper disclosures.[14] By failing to verify that Andrews was the initiator of the requests, Andrews alleged that TRW facilitated the identity theft. She sought injunctive relief, punitive damages and other compensation.

TRW argued that Andrews' claims based on the two earliest disclosures were barred because the Fair Credit Reporting Act's two year statute of limitations had expired.[15] Andrews countered that all of her claims were timely because the statute of limitations did not toll until the date she learned of the inaccurate disclosures. This argument was based upon Andrews' contention that the FCRA incorporated a general

---

[10] *Id.*
[11] 122 S. Ct. 441 (2001).
[12] 122 S. Ct. 445.
[13] *Id.*
[14] *Id.* Not relevant to the Supreme Court's opinion was an additional claim by Andrews that TRW failed to "follow reasonable procedures to assure maximum possible accuracy of the information" in the reports, in violation of 15 U.S.C. 1681e(b). This claim was resolved by a jury in favor of TRW. *Id* at 446, note 3.
[15] 122 S. Ct. at 446.

federal rule which tolls the statute of limitations at the time the plaintiff becomes aware of the injury. The District Court agreed with TRW, and held that a general federal discovery rule was not incorporated into the Fair Credit Reporting Act, thus barring Andrews' claims based on the two earliest disclosures.[16] The District Court also granted TRW's motion for summary judgement on the two remaining claims, finding that TRW had maintained adequate procedures to avoid improper disclosures.[17]

The Ninth Circuit Court of Appeals reversed the District Court, applying the "general federal rule . . . that a federal statue of limitations begins to run when a party knows or has reason to know that she was injured."[18] The Ninth Circuit rejected the District Court's assertion that the text of 15 U.S.C. 1681p, including the exception to the commencement of the statute of limitations, precluded the application of general federal discovery rules, holding that "unless Congress has expressly legislated otherwise the equitable doctrine fo discovery is read into every federal statute of limitations."[19] The court concluded that since the Fair Credit Reporting Act contained no express legislative directive the general rule applied, thus the statute of limitations had not expired on any of Andrews' claims.[20]

TRW appealed to the Supreme Court, which reversed the Ninth Circuit's decision, stating that the Ninth Circuit "conspicuously overstated" the scope and force of the presumption that general discovery rules apply unless Congress has expressly legislated otherwise.[21] The Court said that while some lower federal courts have applied a general discovery rule when a statute is silent on the issue, the Supreme Court has not adopted that position. Furthermore, the Court stated that it had "never endorsed the Ninth Circuit's view that Congress can convey its refusal to adopt a discovery rule only by explicit command, rather than by implication from the structure or text of the particular statute."[22]

While the Ninth Circuit correctly noted that the Fair Credit Reporting Act contains no specific directive against the application of general federal discovery rules, the Court noted that the statute does set forth a specific statute of limitations, along with a single exception to the general rule.[23] Based upon the text and structure of the statute in question, the Supreme Court determined that Congress' "intent to preclude judicial implication of a discovery rule" was clear.[24] Citing an earlier case, the Court held that "[w]here Congress explicitly enumerates certain exceptions to a

---

[16] *Andrews v. Trans Union Corp.*, 7 F. Supp.2d 1056, 1066-1067 (CD Cal. 1998).
[17] 7 F. Supp.2d at 1068-1071.
[18] *Andrews v. TRW*, 225 F.3d 1063, 1066 (9th Cir. 2000).
[19] 225 F.3d at 1067.
[20] *Id.* at 1066.
[21] 122 S. Ct. at 446.
[22] *Id* at 447.
[23] 15 U.S.C. 1681p.
[24] 122 S. Ct. at 447.

general prohibition, additional exceptions are not to be implied, in the absence of evidence of a contrary legislative intent."[25] Applying general principles of statutory construction, the Court reasoned that "Congress implicitly excluded a general discovery rule by explicitly including a more limited one."[26] To allow the incorporation of a general rule in light of this fact, would have the practical effect of rendering the stated exception to the general rule "entirely superfluous in all but the most unusual circumstances," thus violating a "cardinal principal of statutory construction" - that "a statute ought, upon the whole, to be so construed that, if it can be prevented, no clause, sentence, or word shall be superfluous, void or insignificant."[27]

As if anticipating the Court's decision, Andrews argued that if the statute of limitations was to commence on the date on which liability arises, the date should be the date on which the inaccuracies come to the attention of the potential plaintiff, rather than the date on which the credit reporting agency made the inaccurate disclosure.[28] Andrews relied on legislative history pointing to Congress' consideration of alternative language in making her argument. The Court rejected Andrews' reliance on legislative history noting that TRW was able to present information to the contrary.[29] The Court also rejected Andrews' argument that liability did not arise until actual damages materialized. Refusing to address the issue because it was not raised earlier, the Court doubted that the argument would have aided Andrews due to the fact that Andrews' alleged damages began to materialize when the inaccurate disclosures were made, causing the statute of limitations to toll at the same time as under the statutory language in question.[30]

By reversing the Ninth Circuit's decision, the Supreme Court barred Andrews' claims based upon the two earliest disclosures. The case was remanded for further proceedings consistent with the opinion, presumably allowing Andrews to go forward with the other claims.

LEGISLATIVE PROPOSALS

107th Congress

In response to the Supreme Court's opinion, the 107th Congress considered several pieces of legislation which would have allowed more time for victims of

---

[25] *Id.* at 447, *citing* Andrus v. Glover Constr. Co., 446 U.S. 608, 616-617 (1980).
[26] *Id.*
[27] *Id.* at 449 (citations omitted).
[28] *Id.* at 449.
[29] *Id* at 450.
[30] *Id.* at 451.

identity theft to file suit under the Fair Credit Reporting Act. Several of these bills are discussed below. This is not intended to be an exhaustive list of identity theft legislation considered during the 107th Congress.[31]

On November 14, 2002, the Senate passed S. 1742, the Identity Theft Victims Assistance Act of 2002. If enacted, the legislation would have amended the statute of limitations under the FCRA to allow suit to be brought "not later than 2 years from the date of the defendant's violation of any requirement under this title."[32] Actions by victims of identity theft could be brought not later than 4 years from the date of the defendant's violation if the victim "has reasonable grounds to believe that [he or she] is the victim of an identity theft; and has not materially and willfully misrepresented such a claim."[33]

S. 1723, the Protect Victims of Identity Theft Act of 2001, would have also amended the Fair Credit Reporting Act's statute of limitations. The amendment would have allowed suit to be filed "not later than 2 years after the date on which the violation is discovered or should have been discovered by the exercise of reasonable diligence."[34] An identical bill, H.R. 3368, was also introduced.

Another House bill, H.R. 3369, the Fair Credit Reporting Act Amendment of 2001, would have also allowed more time for suit to be filed in cases arising under the Fair Credit Reporting Act. H.R. 3369 would have amended the Act to allow suit to be filed within two years from the "earlier of the date on which the consumer discovers, or the date by which the consumer reasonably should have discovered, the violation giving rise to the liability."[35]

108th Congress

Several bills related to identity theft have been introduced in the 108th Congress. At least two of these bills include a provision to amend the Fair Credit Reporting Act's statute of limitations. To date, no action has been taken on either bill.

S. 22, the Justice Enhancement and Domestic Security Act of 2003, would amend the Fair Credit Reporting Act's statute of limitations generally to allow suit to be brought "not later than 2 years from the date of the defendant's violation of any requirement under [the Act]."[36] In cases where the defendant "materially and willfully misrepresented any information required to be disclosed to an individual," an action may be brought "at any time within 2 years after the date of discovery by the

---

[31] For an overview of legislation related to identity theft, see CRS Report RL31752, *Identity Theft: An Overview of Proposed Legislation*.
[32] S. 1742, as passed, Sec. 4, 107th Cong.
[33] *Id.*
[34] S. 1723, Sec. 2, 107th Cong.
[35] H.R. 3369, Sec. 2, 107th Cong.
[36] S. 22, Sec. 3114, 108th Cong.

individual of the misrepresentation." If the plaintiff is a victim of identity theft, the statute of limitations would be extended to 4 years from the date of the defendant's violation.

H.R. 818, the Identity Theft Consumer Notification Act, would amend the Fair Credit Reporting Act's statute of limitations to allow suit to be brought "not later than 2 years after the date on which the violation is discovered or should have been discovered by the exercise of reasonable diligence."[37]

---

[37] H.R. 818, Sec. 3, 108th Cong.

Chapter 7

PRIVACY PROTECTION FOR CUSTOMER FINANCIAL INFORMATION[†]

M. Maureen Murphy

INTRODUCTION

Title V of the Gramm-Leach-Bliley Act of 1999 (P.L. 106-102, H.Rept. 106-434) requires financial institutions to provide their customers with notice of their privacy policies. It prohibits financial institutions from sharing nonpublic personally identifiable customer information with non-affiliated third parties without giving consumers an opportunity to opt out and prohibits financial institutions from providing account numbers to non-affiliated third parties for marketing purposes. It requires financial institutions to safeguard the security and confidentiality of customer information. Finally, it delegates rulemaking and enforcement authority to the federal banking and security regulators, the Federal Trade Commission, and state insurance regulators. The legislation includes prohibitions on "pretext calling," obtaining financial institution customer information by false pretenses. Legislation has been offered in the 107th Congress to amend these provisions.

[†] Excerpted from CRS Report RS20185. Updated May 10, 2002.

BACKGROUND

With modern technology's ability to gather and retain data, financial services businesses have increasingly found ways to take advantage of their large reservoirs of customer information. Not only can they serve their customers better by tailoring services and communications to their preferences, but they can profit from sharing that information with others willing to pay for customer lists or targeted marketing compilations.[1] While some consumers are pleased with the wider access to information about available services that information sharing among financial services providers offers, others have raised privacy concerns. Individuals are particularly interested in controls on secondary usage.

The United States has no general law of financial privacy. The Constitution, itself, has been held to provide no protection against governmental access to financial information turned over to third parties. *United States v. Miller,* 425 U.S. 435 (1976). This means that although the Fourth Amendment to the United States Constitution requires a search warrant for a government agent to obtain such records as a person's own copies of canceled checks, credit card charges and receipts, loan applications, and stock transfer records, it does not protect the same records when they are held by financial institutions. State constitutions and laws may provide greater protection.

Various federal statutes provide a measure of privacy protection for financial records. The Right to Financial Privacy Act, 12 U.S.C. §§ 3401-3422, sets procedures for federal government access to customer financial records held by financial institutions. The Fair Credit Reporting Act (FCRA), 15 U.S.C. §§ 1681 to 1681t, establishes standards for collection and permissible purposes for dissemination of data by consumer reporting agencies. It also gives consumers access to their files and the right to correct information therein. The Electronic Funds Transfer Act, 15 U.S.C. §§ 1693a to 1693r, describes the rights and liabilities of consumers using electronic fund transfer systems. Among them is the right to have the financial institution provide them with information as to the circumstances under which information concerning their accounts will be disclosed to third parties. With the passage of the Fair Credit Reporting Act Amendments of 1996, P.L. 104-208, Div. A, Tit. II, Subtitle d, Ch. 1, § 2419, 110 *Stat.* 3009-452, adding 15 U.S.C.§ 1681t(b)(2), companies may share with other entities certain customer information respecting their transactions and experience with a customer without any notification requirements. Other customer information, such as credit report or application information, may be shared with other companies in the corporate family if the customers are given "clear and conspicuous"

---

[1] This report addresses financial privacy issues. For more general information on privacy issues see: CRS Report RL30671, *Personal Privacy Protection: The Legislative Response,* by Harold C. Relyea. Also see CRS Issue Brief IB98002, *Medical Records Confidentiality.*

notice about the sharing and an opportunity to direct that the information not be shared.

Gramm-Leach-Bliley's Privacy Provisions

Title V of the Gramm-Leach Bliley Act[2] contains the privacy provisions enacted in conjunction with financial modernization legislation. In addition to strengthening the prohibitions on identity fraud and mandating a federal study on information sharing among financial institutions and their affiliates, the legislation requires that federal regulators issue rules that call for financial institutions to establish standards to insure the security and confidentiality of customer records. It prohibits financial institutions from disclosing nonpublic personal information to unaffiliated third parties without providing customers the opportunity to decline to have such information disclosed. Also included are prohibitions on disclosing customer account numbers to unaffiliated third parties for use in telemarketing, direct mail marketing, or other marketing through electronic mail. Under this legislation financial institutions are required to disclose, initially when a customer relationship is established and annually, thereafter, their privacy policies, including their policies with respect to sharing information with affiliates and non-affiliated third parties.

Rules implementing these privacy provisions have been promulgated by the federal banking and securities regulators. Implementing regulations were published by the banking regulators in the *Federal Register* on June 1, 2000, by the Federal Trade Commission on May 24, and by the SEC on June 29. 65 *Fed. Reg.* 35162, 33646, and 40334.[3] They became effective on November 13, 2000. Compliance was optional until July 1, 2001, meaning that information may be shared after that date provided the necessary steps have been taken by the financial institutions. See FTC regulations at http://www.ftc.gov/privacy/glbact/index.html. Consumers may opt out at any time. Identity theft and pretext calling guidelines were issued to banks on April 6, 2001. [http://www.federalreserve.gov/boarddocs/SRLetters/2001/sr0111.htm].

Insurance industry compliance has been handled on a state-by-state basis by the appropriate state authority. The National Association of Insurance Commissioners (NAIC) approved a model law respecting disclosure of consumer financial and health information intended to guide state legislative efforts in the area.[4]

These privacy provisions preempt state law except to the extent that the state law provides greater protection to consumers. The Federal Trade Commission, in

---

[2] Pub. L. 106-102, tit. v, 113 *Stat.* 1338, 1436. 15 U.S.C. §§ 6801 - 6809. For general information on Gramm-Leach-Bliley, see CRS Report RL30375, *Major Financial Services Legislation, the Gramm-Leach-Bliley Act (P.L. 106-102): an Overview*, by F. Jean Wells and William D. Jackson.

[3] *Federal Register* online at [http://www.access.gpo.gov/su_docs/aces/aces140.html].

[4] [http://www.naic.org/1news/releases]

conjunction with the other federal financial institution regulators, is to make the determination as to whether or not a state law is preempted. The Conference Committee rejected amendments that would have required customers to opt in, i.e., consent, before financial institutions could share customer financial information with either affiliates or third parties.

Privacy issues were discussed at each stage of the legislative process in the House consideration of financial modernization legislation. The House Banking Committee markup of the legislation (H.R. 10, 106th Cong.) included the rejection of an amendment, offered by Representative Inslee, that would have permitted bank customers to preclude sharing their information with third parties. What was accepted instead and included in the bill as reported by the House Banking Committee (H.Rept. 106-74) were provisions that would: require institutions to disclose their privacy policies, mandate a federal privacy study, and prohibit the sharing health information derived from insurance activities. As reported by the House Commerce Committee, H.R. 10's prohibition against sharing individually identified health information derived from insurance activities would have been extended to include genetic information; customers would have been given the opportunity to opt out of information sharing by their financial institutions; and consumers would have been able to examine, upon request, nonpublic personal information before their financial institution shares or sells such information for consideration to nonaffiliated persons or entities.

Public and Industry Reaction

Prior to enactment of Gramm-Leach-Bliley, there were various indicators of the public's interest in financial privacy as well as industry's efforts to address those concerns. One of the indications of the public's interest in preserving the confidentiality of personal information conveyed to financial service providers was the negative reaction to what became an aborted attempt by the federal banking regulators to promulgate "Know Your Customer" rules.[5] These rules would have imposed precisely detailed requirements on banks and other financial institutions to establish profiles of expected financial activity and monitor their customers transactions against these profiles. Even before the Know Your Customer Rules and enactment of Gramm-Leach-Bliley, depository institutions and their regulators have increasingly promoted industry self-regulation as a means of instilling consumer confidence and forestalling comprehensive privacy regulation by state and federal governments. The American Bankers Association, for example, promulgates eight

---

[5] See CRS Report RS20026, *Banking's Proposed 'Know Your Customer' Rules*.

privacy principles for the banking industry,[6] and one of the federal banking regulators, the Office of Comptroller of the Currency, issued an advisory letter regarding information sharing.[7]

The regulatory scheme set in place by Gramm-Leach-Bliley became operative on July 1, 2001. In a certain sense, the debate as to whether information sharing by financial institutions with third parties–outside of their corporate families–should require actual consent rather than an opportunity to opt out continues. Both the FCRA and Gramm-Leach-Bliley contain provisions permitting limited and particularized state preemption of federal standards when state laws provide more protection for consumers. The year 2000 saw activity in some state legislatures considering ways to enhance the protections of Gramm-Leach-Bliley, including requiring actual consent– or opt in–before information sharing Only one state, California, enacted more protective legislation.[8] Industry sources view having to comply with multiple and inconsistent state regimes as posing excessive regulatory costs, litigation prospects, and liability potential. The validity of their claims may be reflected in a position taken by Robert Pitofsky, former Chairman of the Federal Trade Commission, in December 2000, when he went on record as potentially favoring legislation geared towards a nationwide financial privacy standard. In the same speech, however, he indicated that he would also consider enactment of legislation that the industry has resisted: requiring financial services providers to obtain customer consent before sharing data, i.e., an opt-in requirement rather than the current opt-out standard.[9]

A potential issue is the extent of coverage of Gramm-Leach-Bliley. It covers "financial institutions" within the meaning of the Bank Holding Company Act. Many commercial entities that sell or perform services for consumers are not included; some lawyers and accountants may be included because they perform services designated as "financial in nature" either by the BHCA, itself, or by the regulators under authority of that legislation as amended by Gramm-Leach-Bliley. On April 8, 2002, the FTC determined that lawyers were covered and that it had no authority to grant them an exemption; subsequently the New York State Bar Association filed suit.[10]

---

[6] See "Financial Privacy in America: A Review of Consumer Financial Issues," (June 1998). [http://www.aba.com].

[7] "Fair Credit Reporting Act," OCC AL 99-3 (March 29, 1999).

[8] California enacted legislation that requires credit card issuers to provide consumers an opportunity to opt out of information sharing for marketing purposes, includes information sharing with affiliates for marketing purposes, and requires provision of a toll-free telephone number for exercising this right to opt out. 2000 Cal. Stat., ch. 977; 2000 Cal. Adv.Leg. Serv. 977 (Deering).

[9] "FTC Head Favors Federal Action on Privacy, Says Argument for Preemption Now Stronger," 6 *Electronic Commerce & Law Report* 7 (January 3, 2001).

[10] [http://www.nysba.org/Content/ContentGroups/News1/Release_attachments/nysbavftc.pdf]
The American Bar Association had also requested an exemption for attorneys on the grounds that they are subject to stricter confidential requirements under their Code of Professional Responsibility and because having to send out Gramm-Leach-Bliley privacy notices could confuse their clients as to that confidentiality. [http://www.abanet.org/poladv/letters/exec/privacy071001.html].

The European Union Data Directive

Another incentive for a nationwide standard has been the requirements imposed upon companies doing business in Europe under the European Commission on Data Protection (EU Data Directive), an official act of the European Parliament and Council, dated October 24, 1995 (95/46/EC). This imposes strict privacy guidelines respecting the sharing of customer information and barring transfers, even within the same corporate family, outside of Europe, unless the transfer is to a country having privacy laws affording similar protection as does Europe. The Department of Commerce has negotiated an agreement with the European Union that offers a framework under which US companies may be certified by the Department of Commerce and obtain a safe harbor, thereby continuing data transfers.[11] To date, the banking industry has not availed itself of this safe harbor, nor has the EU accepted Gramm-Leach-Bliley as one of the safe harbors meeting the Data Directive's requirements. U.S. entities with a presence in Europe, including some of the large bank holding companies, have chosen to draft guidelines and codes of conduct to meet the European standard and to satisfy that standard through separate negotiations. U.S. companies also have the option of adopting a standard contract approved in June 2001 by the European Commission, despite U.S. objections, for foreign companies to use to comply with the EU Data Directive.

Legislation

In the 107th Congress, Title III of P.L. 107-56, the USA PATRIOT Act, includes various amendments to the anti-money laundering laws and requires closer scrutiny of accounts held in the name of foreign banks. S. 420, the Bankruptcy Reform Act of 2001, as reported and as passed by the Senate, includes a provision for the appointment of a privacy ombudsman in a bankruptcy proceeding to provide the court with information about the privacy policy of a debtor and its implication in any sale of the debtor's customer lists.

S. 2201 (Sen. Hollings) apples to online businesses; requires notice, affirmative consent (opt-in) for sensitive personally identifiable information, and an opt-out for other personally identifiable information; and includes a consumer right to correct information and judicial remedies for violations. H.R. 4678 (Rep. Stearns) applies to businesses in general, requires notice, includes an opt-out and a program of self-regulation administered by the FTC. Both bills would preempt state law. Other legislation includes : S. 30 (Sen. Sarbanes), amending Gramm-Leach-Bliley to require consumer consent for disclosure by financial institutions of certain data, extend the

---

[11] See Department of Commerce website: [http://www.ita.doc.gov/].

opt-out requirements to data sharing among affiliates, and authorize consumer access and correction of information; S. 324 (Sen. Shelby), specifying that Social Security numbers are non-public personal information for Gramm-Leach-Bliley privacy purposes; S. 450 (Sen. Nelson), requiring opt-in for sharing of health information, opt-out for sharing information with affiliates, and enhancing enforcement mechanisms; S. 536 (Sen. Shelby), requiring an option for sharing profiling or marketing information; S. 1055 (Sen. Feinstein), requiring an opt-out for commercial entities' sale of personally identifiable information to nonaffiliated third parties, amending Gramm-Leach-Bliley to require an opt-in in instances of disclosure for marketing purposes or sale of non-public personally identifiable information and to limit the exceptions to its nondisclosure provision, limiting the use of social security numbers, adding protections for driver's license information, and limiting disclosure of certain health information; H.R. 583 (Reps. Hutchinson and Moran), establishing a privacy commission; H.R. 1478 (Rep. Kleczka), prohibiting unconsented use of social security numbers; H.R. 2036 (Rep. Shaw), restricting the use of the social security number in public and private sectors; H.R. 2135 (Rep. Sawyer), requiring and opt-in for sharing consumer information; H.R. 2720 (Markey), requiring consumer consent (opt-in) for disclosure or unrelated use–even to affiliates–of nonpublic personal information collected by a financial institution in connection with any consumer transaction, prohibiting financial institutions from denying service to consumers who fail to provide such consent, providing consumers with a right to examine their data, prohibiting the disclosure of account numbers to affiliates or consumer reporting agencies for marketing purposes, authorizing the chief law enforcement officer of each state to bring a civil enforcement action in federal court, allowing each functional regulator to rule on state preemption issues, broadening the definition of "financial institution," and requiring states to elect as to whether to establish privacy rules for insurance industry; H.R. 2730 (Rep. Sessions), preempting states from imposing requirements or prohibitions on financial institutions other than those found in Gramm-Leach-Bliley's substantive privacy provisions and the regulations pertaining thereto, and making permanent the FCRA's current preemption–scheduled to end January 1, 2004–of state laws restricting sharing of credit report information among affiliates; and, H.R. 3068 (Rep. Ney), establishing a commission on financial privacy and national security.

House Energy and Commerce Committee hearings included such diverse topics as: the EU Data Protection Directive: Implications in the U.S. Privacy Debate; Privacy in the Commercial World; and Existing Federal Statutes Addressing Information Privacy [http://energycommerce.house.gov/ 107/action/action.htm].

The FCRA provisions on affiliate sharing of information preempt state law until January 1, 2004. Subsection (b)(2) of section 624, 15 U.S.C. § 1681t(b)(2), provides a general exception to the FCRA's general rule on preemption. Under that rule, FCRA does not preempt state law, unless the state law is inconsistent, and then it is preempted only to the extent of the inconsistency.[12] An exception to this rule applies to sharing of information among affiliates.[13] States may override this exception after January 1, 2004, by implementing or enacting laws providing greater protection to consumers with respect to information sharing among affiliates.[14] Gramm-Leach-Bliley, on the other hand, preempts state laws to the extent that they are inconsistent but provides that "a State statute, regulation, order, or interpretation is not inconsistent ... if the protection such statute, regulation, order, or interpretation affords any person is greater than the protection under this subtitle as determined by the Federal Trade Commission...."[15] States may provide greater protection to consumers than Gramm-Leach-Bliley at any time. The FCRA moratorium ends on January 1, 2004.

---

[12] 15 U.S.C. § 1681t(a).
[13] 15 U.S.C. § 1681t(b)(2).
[14] 15 U.S.C. § 1681t(d)(2).
[15] 15 U.S.C. §§ 6824(b), Pub. L. 106-102, § 524(b), 113 *Stat.* 1448.

Chapter 8

SOCIAL SECURITY IDENTITY THEFT FACT SHEET

Quick Facts About Social Security *Identity Theft*

- The Social Security Administration (SSA) estimates that over 290 million Americans currently have Social Security numbers (SSNs). According to the Federal Trade Commission, SSNs are a principal component used to commit identity theft.
- Identity theft is considered the fastest growing financial crime in the country - affecting an estimated 500,000-700,000 people annually.
- Allegations received by the SSA Hotline involving potential fraudulent SSN use for identity theft increased from 62,000 cases in fiscal year 1999 to over 90,000 in fiscal year 2000 - **almost a 50 percent increase** in just one year.

Identity Theft Costs Millions Each Year

- Actual losses to individuals and institutions rose from $442 million in 1995 to $745 million in 1997 - a 169% increase in just two years.
- Identity theft victims spend 2 years trying to remove an average $18,000 in fraudulent charges from their credit reports.
- 34% of consumers who reported the dollar amount that the thief had obtained by using their identities reported an amount of $1,000 or less; 35% reported an amount between $1,001 and $5,000; 13% reported an amount between $5,001 and $10,000; and 18% reported an amount greater than $10,000.

- Two major insurance companies have begun offering identity and credit card theft insurance due to the increase in identity theft as well as concerns expressed by their customers.
- More than 75% of identity theft crimes last year involved victims of "true name" fraud. This occurs when someone uses the SSN to open new accounts in the victim's name.
- The average amount of time it took victims to resolve their cases was nearly 2 years (23 months). Victims who were not able to resolve their cases within two years were still dealing with the problem for an average of 44 months.
- Victims spent an average of 175 hours and $808 in out-of-pocket costs (not including lawyer's fees) trying to fix their problem.

Identity Theft is Prevalent

The following are the most common types of identity theft complaints reported by consumers[1]:

- **Credit Card Fraud:** 47% of consumers reported that a credit card account was opened in their name or unauthorized charges were placed on their existing credit card.
- **Unauthorized Phone or Utility Services:** 22% of consumers reported that the identity thief had established new telephone, cellular, or other utility service in their name.
- **Bank Fraud:** 15% of consumers reported that a new bank account had been opened in their name, fraudulent checks had been written, or unauthorized withdrawals had been made from their account.
- **Fraudulent Loans:** 8% of consumers reported that the identity thief had obtained a loan (personal, business, auto, real estate, etc.) in their name.
- **Government Documents or Benefits:** 8% of consumers reported that the identity thief had obtained government documents or benefits in their name.
- **Multiple Types:** Approximately 50% of the consumers reported experiencing more than one of the above types of identity theft.

---

[1] Source: Social Security Administration's Office of Inspector General, Federal Trade Commission, Privacy Rights Clearing House, California Public Interest Group

H.R. 2036 - SOCIAL SECURITY NUMBER PRIVACY AND IDENTITY THEFT PREVENTION ACT OF 2001

Social Security Number (SSN) Protections in the Public Sector

Prohibits Federal, State and local governments from:

- selling SSNs (limited exceptions are made to facilitate law enforcement and national security, to ensure the accuracy of credit and insurance underwriting information, and to allow for the effective administration of programs authorized under the Social Security Act),
- displaying SSNs to the general public and on Internet sites (limited exceptions are made to facilitate law enforcement and national security and to ensure the accuracy of credit information),
- displaying SSNs on checks issued for payment,
- displaying SSNs on drivers' licenses, motor vehicle registrations or other identification documents issued by State Departments of Motor Vehicles,
- displaying SSNs on visible employee identification cards or military tags, and
- employing prisoners in jobs that provide them with access to SSNs.
- Strengthens verification requirements for birth records when someone applies for a SSN card.
- Requires the Commissioner of Social Security and the Attorney General to report on the progress of the Social Security Administration and the Immigration and Naturalization Service in implementing a process for enumeration of aliens who are in need of SSNs.

Social Security Number Protections in the Private Sector

- Authorizes the Attorney General to issue regulations restricting the display, sale and purchase of SSNs in the private sector (limited exceptions including for law enforcement, including child support enforcement, and national security, public health, health or safety emergency situations, research, individual's written consent, and as deemed appropriate by the Attorney General).

- Prohibits a person from obtaining another person's SSN to locate or identify the individual with the intent to physically injure, harm, or use the individual's identity for an illegal purpose.

- Discourages businesses from denying services to individuals who refuse to provide their SSNs by subjecting them to penalties under Federal law (limited exception for businesses required by Federal law to submit individual's SSN to Federal government).

- Includes the SSN in the definition of "credit report" under the Fair Credit Reporting Act so that the SSN receives the same privacy protections as other consumer credit information.

Enforcement

- Creates new criminal (up to 5 years imprisonment and fine up to $250,000) and civil penalties (up to $5,000 for each incident) for violations of the law relating to display, sale, purchase, misuse of the SSN, or offering to acquire, for a fee, an additional SSN.

NEW PRIVACY PROTECTIONS FOR BANK CUSTOMERS

Congressmen Jerry Kleczka and Paul Ryan introduced a bill that will make sure customers are notified as soon as possible if their bank discovers that their personal financial information has been stolen.

Kleczka, a long-time proponent of privacy protection, sponsored the *Identity Theft* Consumer Notification Act (HR 5474) after it was discovered that over 250 bank customers had personal information stolen in southeastern Wisconsin. Compounding the violation was the fact that the customers were not told that their personal and financial records had been compromised until eight months after bank officials learned of the theft.

In the meantime, those whose information had been stolen had no idea that it had been sold to a ring of identity thieves who were using the financial records to make purchases in the victims' names, including high-end automobiles.

"Financial institutions owe it to their customers to quickly tell them if their privacy has been violated so they can take steps to minimize risks to their finances and repair any damage that has been done," Kleczka said. "Identity theft undermines one's sense of security and those banks we regularly trust with this important information have a duty to help their customers who are victimized because of breaches in security."

"If a bank's safeguards have been breached and customers' personal information has been compromised, customers have a right to know about it," Ryan said. "All of us count on our financial institutions to protect our confidential data. If there's a breakdown in their privacy protections, we need to find out right away so we can protect our credit and take action to protect ourselves."

The bill requires financial institutions to promptly notify customers of any compromise in the security of their personal information and provide assistance to such customers in correcting any damage to their credit ratings. These banks also would have to reimburse the customer for any losses incurred as a result of the identity theft. Once a year, financial institutions would be required to notify their customers of these rights in writing.

Financial institutions also would face a number of penalties if they fail to notify customers in a timely manner. These penalties could include the removal of loss of status as a federally insured deposit institution as well as civil fines. However, in order to protect an active investigation, law enforcement officials would be able to request a temporary waiver of disclosure from these regulations.

"Identity theft is often a silent, hidden crime until the information is used to purchase goods or services in the victim's name. By then it is too late, and the victims have to face the difficulty of clearing their names and recovering their good credit history," Kleczka said. "This bill will help reduce the long-term effects of identity theft by ensuring that customers know as soon as possible when their personal information has been compromised. With this knowledge they can take steps to protect their finances and credit."

PREVENTING *IDENTITY THEFT*

Identity theft occurs when an individual uses personal information such as the name, date of birth or the Social Security Number of another person without permission. Identity thieves use the personal information to commit fraud. Incidences of identity theft have increased in recent years, and it is a frightening ordeal for anyone who has had their personal information stolen.

An identity thief can open a new credit card account, using someone else's personal information. When they use the credit card and don't pay the bills, the delinquent account is reported on the victim's credit report. Identity thieves can also call a credit card issuer, pretend to be someone else, and change the mailing address on the credit card account. Because the bills are not sent to the owner of the credit card it could take some time for the owner to realize that there is a problem. A bank account can also be opened by an identify thief who can then write bad checks using someone else's information.

According to the Federal Trade Commission the following steps can be taken to minimize identity thief by managing personal information wisely.

- Before revealing personal identifying information, find out how it will be used and if it will be shared with others.
- Pay attention to billing cycles. Follow up with creditors if bills do not arrive on time.
- Minimize the identification information and credit cards carried to what is actually needed.
- Order a credit report every year and make sure it is accurate.

If a person believes that his personal information has been stolen he should take the following three steps. First, contact the three major credit bureaus, Equifax, Experian and Trans Union, and tell them to flag the file with a fraud alert, including a statement that creditors should get permission before opening any new accounts. Second, contact the creditors for any accounts that have been tampered with or opened fraudulently and ask to speak to someone in the fraud department. Third, file a report with the local police or the police in the community where the identity theft took place. Keep a copy of the police report in case creditors need proof of the crime.

Often, each of these agencies will require separate forms to begin disputing fraudulent debts and accounts. To simplify the lengthy filing process, the Federal Trade Commission (FTC) has created the ID Theft Affidavit. Instead of completing different forms, the FTC affidavit can be used by credit bureaus, creditors and police departments.

To combat identity theft I strongly supported the passage of the ***Identity Theft*** and Assumption Deterrence Act of 1998. This measure makes it a federal crime when anyone knowingly transfers or uses, without lawful authority, a means of identification of another person with the intent to commit, or to aid or abet, any unlawful activity that constituents a violation of Federal law, or that constitutes a felony under any applicable state law.

I am also an original co-author of the ***Identity Theft*** Protection and Information Blackout Act of 2003. If enacted, this measure would institute uniform national safeguards on the collection, use, display and confidentiality of an individual's Social Security number by the government and private entities.

INDEX

A

access through relationship with victim, 35, 36
account number, 4, 10, 77
aggravated identity theft, 8, 80
alleged theft, 78, 79
American Bankers Association (ABA), 21, 22, 47-49, 52, 53, 87, 140
anonymity, 58
armed forces, 121
arrests, 21, 39, 40, 43, 44, 46, 68, 102-105
attempt to collect, 76
Attorney General, 2, 3, 5, 7, 9, 10, 14, 27, 58, 94, 95, 96, 98, 100, 104, 105, 107, 110, 112, 114, 115, 120, 147
awareness, 20, 24, 29, 34, 46, 55, 66, 96, 110, 116, 117, 122

B

bank accounts, 21, 47, 58, 73, 114
bank and wire fraud, 8
bank customers, 140, 148
bank officials, 51, 52, 54, 60, 148
banking account number, 68
billing error(s), 76
blocking, 7, 8, 80
Bureau of Prisons (BOP), 26, 71

C

California Public Interest Research Group (CALPIRG), 24, 66
cellular telephones, 111
chat rooms, 57
child support, 4, 130, 147
children, 111, 115
civil and criminal penalties, 86
civil damages, 78
civil monetary penalties, 3, 5, 10, 124
civil penalties, 4, 77, 148
claimants, 79
claims, 8, 42, 76, 79, 131-133, 141
Clinton, President, 46
collateral, 116
commerce, 18, 23, 47, 59, 61, 74, 75, 81, 130
commercial entities, 81, 141, 143
Commissioner of Social Security, 2, 13, 128, 147
community service, 26
community supervision, viii, 25, 26, 68, 72
compliance, 91, 139
comprehensive privacy regulation, 140
computer intrusions (hacking), 111
computers, 43, 115, 119, 120
confidentiality, ix, 13, 75, 86, 119, 120, 126, 130, 137, 139-141, 150

congressional hearing, 34, 58, 59, 100, 111, 118
consumer complaint(s), vii, 1, 6, 19, 28, 67, 82, 95, 119
consumer confidence, 18, 21, 23, 47, 57, 59, 60, 140
consumer credit report, 79
consumer credit, vii, 1, 6, 11, 12, 20, 32, 75, 76, 78, 84, 86, 88, 90, 130, 148
consumer education programs, 27, 107, 115
consumer information, 8, 14, 86, 90, 143
Consumer Privacy Protection Act, 14, 81
consumer reporting agenc(y)ies, viii, 5-7, 12, 18-21, 23, 29, 75, 78-80, 82-84, 86, 87, 130, 138, 143
consumer reporting agencies (CRAs), 29, 30, 52, 54, 55, 56
consumer(s) report(s), 3, 5, 6, 9, 11, 15, 62, 78, 80, 82, 83, 87, 86, 90, 130
consumer's account, 76, 77
convicted offenders, 102
cost of investigations, 69, 70
Council on White Collar Crime, 27, 115
coworker, 32, 35, 36
credit bureaus, 18, 28, 90, 150
credit card account numbers, 10, 111
credit card accounts, 28, 67, 111
credit card issuers, 5, 19, 28, 80, 82, 83, 141
credit card numbers, vii, 1, 6, 78, 80, 82
credit card-issuing banks, 47, 51, 59
credit cards, 21, 37, 41, 44, 45, 47, 49, 52, 58, 59, 68, 73, 78, 97, 101, 105, 113, 128, 150
credit files, 29, 30, 31, 33, 56, 57, 75
credit grantors, 20, 29
credit records, viii, 68, 73
credit report(s), vii, 2, 6, 7, 56, 62, 67, 68, 75, 78-80, 82, 84, 87, 88, 90, 127, 130, 131, 138, 143, 145, 148-150
credit reporting agency, 5, 7, 75, 79, 85, 130, 131, 133
credit unions, 27
credit-card fraud, 58

creditor, 31, 62, 76
crime victims, 68
criminal convictions, 26, 96, 122, 125
criminal financial activity, 44
criminal justice administrators, 26, 94
criminal justice system, viii, 18, 25, 68, 99
criminal penalties, vii, viii, 1, 2, 5, 9, 10, 73
criminal prosecution, 78, 105
criminal record, 66, 67
criminal sanctions, 4
criminals, 40, 43-45, 57, 68, 94
customer financial information, 27, 89, 140
customer information, ix, 86-90, 137, 138, 142
cyberspace, 57

D

damaged credit, 66, 73
data collection, 14
date of birth, vii, viii, 17, 68, 79, 93, 149
debit card, 77, 83
deceptive act, 11, 13, 83
Department of Commerce, 23, 59, 60, 142
Department of Defense, 121
Department of Justice/Justice Department, 13, 18, 27, 29, 39, 58, 69, 94, 96, 98, 100, 101, 107, 109, 113, 115, 120, 122
Department of State/State Department, 27, 112, 147
Department of the Treasury, 18, 29, 42, 94
disclosure, 4, 11, 27, 75, 81, 84, 86, 87, 89, 90, 130, 133, 139, 142, 149
disputed amount, 76
District of Columbia, 34, 111, 118
documentation, 18, 33, 77, 94, 99, 106
dollar losses, 42, 49, 50, 63
driver's license, 67, 74, 81, 100, 114, 143
drug trafficking, 75

E

e-commerce, 21, 23, 47, 57-60, 111

economic growth, 59
education programs, 27, 107, 115
education, 27, 107, 115
electronic commerce, 59
electronic crimes, 110, 111
Electronic Fund Transfer Act (EFTA), 76
electronic fund transfers, 76, 77
electronic monitoring, 26, 72
electronic terminal, 77
e-mail, 57, 121
e-merchants, 58
emergency situations, 4, 13, 147
employment, 35, 38, 62, 64, 65, 86, 104, 113
European Union (EU), 58, 91, 142, 143
Executive Office for U.S. Attorneys (EOUSA), 18, 19, 26, 39, 40, 71, 94, 100
express written authorization, 11, 82

F

face-to-face transaction, 58
Fair Credit Billing Act (FCBA), 76
Fair Credit Reporting Act (FCRA), viii, 1, 3, 5-7, 9-12, 16, 75, 80-91, 127, 129-132, 134, 135, 138, 141, 143, 148
false pretenses, 8, 98, 137
false statements, 8
family member(s), 35, 36, 51
family, 51, 52, 85, 87, 138, 142
federal agencies, 18, 25, 68, 93, 112, 119
federal and state laws, 26
Federal Bureau of Investigation (FBI), 18, 19, 21, 25, 39-41, 69, 93, 94, 102, 109, 112, 113, 116, 119
federal crime, 17, 74, 150
Federal Deposit Insurance Corporation (FDIC), 23, 27, 60
federal government employees, 4
federal offenders, 26, 71, 72
federal prosecutors, 26, 94, 100, 101
Federal Trade Commission(FTC), 1, 2, 5, 6, 11-14, 18, 29, 73, 81-83, 88, 94, 137, 139, 141, 144-146, 150

felony, 8, 74, 77, 78, 80, 96, 98, 101, 104, 105, 108, 126, 150
fictitious addresses, 111
finance charges, 76
finances, 148, 149
financial and electronic crimes, 27, 110
financial crime, 145
Financial Crimes Enforcement Network (FinCEN), 42, 44, 45
financial identity theft, 78
financial institution(s), viii, 15, 17, 21-23, 27, 44, 45, 49-51, 57, 58, 60, 62, 67, 70, 76, 77, 81, 85-90, 118, 137-143, 149
financial privacy laws, 89
financial services, viii, 18, 21, 24, 28, 47, 58, 61, 62, 67, 138, 141
firearms, 19, 40, 100
foreign commerce, 74
Fourth Amendment, 138
fraud alerts, 6, 19, 20, 29, 31, 33, 56, 57, 78, 80, 83
fraud losses, 18, 21, 22, 44, 47, 50-52, 54
fraudulent activities, 24, 52, 57, 64-66, 95, 109
fraudulent identification documents, viii, 73
fraudulent products and services, 57
fraudulent schemes, 27
fraudulent transaction(s), 57, 58, 60, 79, 111
FTC, 5, 18, 20, 24, 27, 28, 29, 33, 34, 35, 36, 43, 58, 61, 62, 63, 65, 81, 88, 94, 95, 96, 98, 106, 107, 110, 116, 117, 118, 119, 120, 121, 122, 125, 126, 139, 141, 142, 150
full disclosure, 11
funding, 11

G

General Accounting Office, 17, 28, 93
government and private entities, 150
government documents, 81, 146
governmental agencies, 3
governmental agency, 4

Gramm-Leach-Bliley Act (GLBA), viii, 9, 15, 27, 85-90, 137, 139

H

health, 2, 4, 9, 13, 62, 72, 81, 139, 140, 143, 147
heroin, 108
hotline reporting, 18, 28
House Committee on Ways and Means, 11, 12, 68
House Energy and Commerce Committee, 143
House of Representatives, 8
housing, 6, 38, 64, 65, 91, 112

I

identification documents, 17, 74, 78, 96, 97, 126, 127, 147
identification, viii, 3, 4, 8, 9, 11, 17, 21, 31, 33, 35, 43, 44, 64, 65, 68, 73, 74, 78, 80, 82, 83, 96, 97, 99, 101, 113, 114, 117, 126-128, 147, 150
identifying information, 6, 11, 36, 49, 58, 82, 99, 105, 115
Identity Theft Act, viii, 6, 12, 17, 19, 27, 93, 94, 96, 97, 100-102, 105, 115-117, 125, 126, 134
identity theft activities, 18, 65, 77
identity theft affidavit(s), 14, 81
Identity Theft and Financial Privacy Act, 82
Identity Theft Consumer Notification Act, 15, 81, 135, 148
identity theft crimes, 54, 69, 93-95, 100, 103, 109, 146
Identity Theft Data Clearinghouse, 20, 24, 27, 33, 34, 95, 96, 117, 119, 120, 122, 123, 125, 126
Identity Theft Penalty Enhancement Act, 8, 16, 80
Identity Theft Prevention Act, 4, 5, 12, 80, 81, 147
identity theft prevention, 14, 81

Identity Theft Protection and Information Blackout Act, 83, 150
identity theft statute(s), 26, 76, 77, 79, 95, 98, 102-106, 108, 109
identity theft victims, 18, 24, 34, 61-63, 65, 66, 95, 106, 117, 118, 120, 126
identity theft-related losses, viii, 21, 22, 50, 51
identity theft-related statistics, 20, 39, 42
identity thieves, 43, 54, 58, 114, 148
illegal activities, 27
Immigration and Nationality Act, 9
Immigration and Naturalization Service (INS), 38, 112, 147
immigration law, 99
immigration, 97, 99, 101
impostors, 74, 77, 78
imprisonment, viii, 26, 72, 74, 80, 93, 100, 102, 108, 127, 128, 148
incarceration, viii, 25, 26, 68
incentive, 108, 142
income, 42, 65, 77
increase in crimes, 68
increasing costs, viii, 21
industry self-regulation, 140
information sharing, viii, 7, 85, 86, 89, 90, 138-141, 144
inmate, 3, 9, 26, 71, 114
Inspector General, 18, 29, 37, 69, 94, 96, 122, 125, 146
insurance companies, 22, 27, 51, 87, 90, 146
integrity, 25
intelligence, 118, 121
intent to commit, 74, 96, 126, 127, 150
interests of the consumer, 82
Internal Revenue Service (IRS), 18, 42, 64, 94, 109
International Association of Chiefs of Police (IACP), 27, 102, 106, 107, 115, 116, 122
International Chamber of Commerce's Commercial Crime Service, 58
international terrorism, 75
internet fraud, 58

internet, 7, 13, 17, 21, 23, 28, 35, 38, 43, 45, 47, 48, 57-60, 83, 93, 105, 111, 113, 147
Internet-related securities fraud, 58
interpretation, 144
interstate commerce, 81
investigative report, 79
investment advisers, 27
investment companies, 27, 101
investment schemes, 58

J

jail time, 77
judicial recourse, 78
junk mail, 57
Justice Enhancement and Domestic Security Act, 80, 134

K

Kleczka, 143, 148, 149
Kleczka, Congressmen Jerry, 148
know fraud initiative, 46
knowing and willful violations, 4
known victims, 18, 28

L

law enforcement agencies, vii, 19, 21, 29, 45, 69, 94-96, 99, 100, 102, 104, 106, 107, 109-112, 114, 116, 117, 119, 120, 122, 123, 125
leadership, 27, 110, 115
limited exceptions, 4, 80, 147
loans, 28, 43, 58, 67, 68, 106, 114
local government, 2, 25, 147

M

mandatory minimum sentence, 108
marketing information, 143
MasterCard, 18, 22, 47, 49, 50, 51
media, 32
mental health, 72

methodology, 25, 69, 70, 71
minimum-security facilities, 26
misdemeanor, 98, 108
missing and exploited children, 111
modernization, 139, 140
money laundering, 44
money, 22, 23, 44, 47-49, 53, 68, 98
mortgages, 58
multiple methods of obtaining data, 35

N

name, address, and telephone number, 11
National Association of Attorneys General, 27, 102, 115
National Association of Insurance Commissioners (NAIC), 139
National District Attorneys Association, 27, 102, 115, 116
national security, 2, 4, 9, 13, 143, 147
Negative Credit Notification Act, 82
negative payment history, 68
neighbor, 32, 35
new technology, 51
New York City, 34, 68
New York Police Department, 111

O

Office of the Comptroller of the Currency (OCC), 27, 67, 68, 141
Office of the Inspector General (OIG), 18, 20, 24, 25, 27-29, 34-38, 62, 69-71, 94, 96, 99, 109, 114, 116, 117, 119, 122-126
often-quoted estimates, 18, 28
online auction schemes, 58
online banking, 59, 60
online transactions, 59, 60
opportunity costs, 54
organized crime, 52, 110

P

passports, 8, 97

PATRIOT Act, 142
payment card associations, 18, 21, 22, 47
payment card number, 59
payment-card fraud, 58
personal (and) financial information, 68, 81, 148
personal and financial records, 148
personal identification card, 4
personal identifying information, vii, viii, 6, 17, 93, 105, 115, 150
Personal Information Privacy Act, 11, 82
personal information, 11, 15, 20, 27, 29, 34, 35, 43, 45, 51, 64, 65, 68, 81, 82, 85, 86, 88, 90, 95, 99, 103, 105, 109, 113, 139, 140, 143, 148, 149, 150
personally identifiable information, ix, 81, 142
police department(s), 95, 105-109, 116, 118, 120, 150
police report, 24, 33, 66, 79, 106, 107, 150
police, 18, 24, 28, 33, 65, 66, 68, 79, 95, 102, 105-109, 116, 118, 120-122, 150
policymakers, 26, 94
potential fraud, 5, 82
prevalent method, 35
prevention of identity theft, 33, 81, 117
prevention provisions, 80
Privacy Act, 2, 81, 138
privacy of the individual, 4, 13
privacy policies, ix, 86, 87, 137, 139, 140
privacy protection, 14, 138, 148
Privacy Rights Clearinghouse, 24, 66, 67
private sector, 4, 19, 83, 95, 110-112, 116, 143, 147
probation, 26, 72, 105, 124
profiling, 143
prohibition, 2-4, 9, 83, 86, 87, 133, 140
proliferation, 43
proof of purchase, 76
proof of the crime, 150
public assistance, 10
public health, 2, 4, 9, 13, 147
public knowledge, 4, 13
public records, 2, 4, 9, 80
public sector, 147

R

racketeering, 114
refund crimes, 42
refunds, 42, 62, 65, 66
registration, 3, 9, 10
regulation, 13, 86, 144
Right to Financial Privacy Act, 138

S

Secret Service, 18, 19, 21, 25, 27, 28, 42-44, 49, 69, 70, 93, 94, 107, 109-113, 116-120, 122
Secretary of the Treasury, 86
Securities and Exchange Commission, 58
security alert, 31, 32, 56, 78
security and privacy, 21, 23, 60
Senate Committee on Finance, 5
Senate, 2, 3, 5-8, 10, 80, 89-91, 118, 134, 142
September 11, 116
service providers, 140
Social Security Act, 2, 4, 5, 9, 10, 147
Social Security Administration (SSA), 5, 10, 18, 20, 24, 25, 27-29, 34-38, 62, 69-71, 94, 96, 99, 109, 112, 114, 116, 117, 119, 122-126, 145-147
Social Security Number Misuse Prevention Act, 80
Social Security Numbers (SSNs), vii, viii, 2-5, 9, 10, 12, 13, 17, 20, 25, 29, 36-39, 41, 43, 52, 68-71, 73, 93, 94, 96, 97, 99, 101, 113, 115, 122-126, 128, 143, 145-149
social security, vii, 1, 9, 79-81, 83, 131, 143
spam, 57
state agencies, 25
state and local law enforcement, 27, 93, 94, 119, 126
state law, 74, 85-89, 102, 139, 142, 143, 150
state or local law, 74, 124

Index 157

statistics, 17, 19, 21, 25, 28-30, 32, 33, 39-43, 45, 46, 49, 68, 96, 100, 104-106, 120, 122, 124
stolen personal identity information, 109
substance abuse treatment, 26, 72
Supreme Court, viii, 107, 129, 131-133
suspicious activity reports (SAR), 44, 45

T

task forces, 27, 95, 110-112, 119
taxes, 64
technology, 21, 23, 45, 57, 59, 60, 105, 112, 138
telecommunications fraud, 111
telecommunications, 97, 111
terrorism, 75, 80
the Know Your Customer Rules, 140
threat, 48
transaction information, 7, 79, 88
transportation, 126

U

U.S. Postal Inspection Service, 45, 46
unauthorized charges, 73, 75-77, 146
unauthorized transactions, 76
unauthorized transfers, 77

unemployment benefits, 65
unemployment, 65
Uniform Crime Reporting (UCR), 102
unions, 27
United States Constitution, 138
unlawful activity, 74, 96, 127, 150
unsolicited commercial e-mail (spam), 57

V

validity, 69, 141
verification of birth records, 4
victims of identity theft, viii, 6, 8, 14, 20, 29, 36, 61, 66-68, 73, 78, 79, 81-83, 106, 107, 116, 129, 134
violation of federal law, 74
violence, 75
violent crime, 95, 108, 110
Visa, 18, 22, 47, 49-1, 59

W

white-collar crime, 25, 26, 58, 69, 71, 101
without lawful authority, 8, 74, 80, 96, 150
written confirmation, 79
written consent, 11, 82, 89, 147
written notice from the consumer, 77
written proof, 76